The Bible Promise
Life Recovery™ Devotional

LIFE RECOVERY

DEVOTIONAL

*A Promise Each Day
of Hope, Strength, and Courage*

WIGHTMAN WEESE

Tyndale House Publishers, Inc.
Wheaton, Illinois

Library of Congress Cataloging-in-Publication Data

The Bible Promise Life Recovery Devotional.
    p. cm.
  ISBN 0-8423-3810-1
   1. Twelve-step programs—Religious aspects—Christianity—Meditations. 2. Bible—Meditations. 3. Devotional calendars.
I. Tyndale House Publishers.
BL624.5.B53   1992
242'.4—dc20   92-11330

Printed in the United States of America

98 97 96 95 94 93 92
8   7   6   5   4   3   2   1

Contents

F I V E Dealing with Attitudes

S I X A New Start

S E V E N Making Good Choices

E I G H T Finding Sources of Strength

N I N E Looking Better to Ourselves

T E N Dealing with Temptation

E L E V E N Living with the Consequences

T W E L V E Thinking of Others

Introduction

❧ When God wanted to make himself known to Abraham, he called himself *El Shaddai,* a name the patriarchs associated with God as a covenant-keeper. God keeps his promises!

❧ His name *El Shaddai* also identifies him as all-sufficient, or as others have defined the term, "the God who is more than enough." What God promises, he can do!

❧ Here are 360 promises from our promise-keeping God, each one a valuable resource to use in facing whatever the day might bring our way. There are twelve sections—one for each month of the year, and there are thirty readings in each section—almost one for each day of the month.

❧ Read them and revel in them; claim the promises and celebrate the providence of God—one a day, or as many each day as it takes to convince you that God is good and that he has our welfare in mind.

Part One

God Will Take Away Our Guilt

*Therefore, my brothers, I
want you to know that
through Jesus the forgiveness
of sins is proclaimed to you.
Through him everyone who
believes is justified from
everything you could not be
justified from by the law of
Moses.* Acts 13:38-39

> **Good things can happen when we admit we have failed.**

"I will set out and go back to my father and say to him: Father, I have sinned against heaven and against you. . . ." But while he was still a long way off, his father saw him and was filled with compassion for him; he ran to his son, threw his arms around him and kissed him. . . . The father said to his servants, ". . . Let's have a feast and celebrate. For this son of mine was dead and is alive again; he was lost and is found."

Luke 15:18-24

At one time or another, we have all felt like this person we call the Prodigal Son. But God has never stopped watching the road, waiting for us to come back to him so he can forgive us, restore us, and show us how much he loves us. It is never too late to come back home.

> **God loves us—not less, but
> perhaps even more—when we
> admit how much we need him.**

*Blessed are the poor in spirit, for theirs is the
kingdom of heaven.*   Matthew 5:3

To be poor in spirit is to admit how powerless
and spiritually bankrupt we are. We are never
so weak or poor as when we think we can run
our life without God's help. We are on the road
to becoming strong and spiritually prosperous
when we admit to God how much we need him.

> **God comes to our rescue when
> we admit we are vulnerable.**

*Let men cast off their wicked deeds; let them
banish from their minds the very thought of
doing wrong! Let them turn to the Lord that he
may have mercy upon them, and to our God, for
he will abundantly pardon!*   Isaiah 55:7; TLB

Nothing we ever did was hidden from God.
Shame causes us to either deny our problem or
try to hide it from others. Help comes for our
weakness when we accept the forgiveness God
offers us as we return to him.

> **Denial and pride are great
> enemies of our recovery.**

*If we claim to be without sin, we deceive our-
selves and the truth is not in us. If we confess
our sins, he is faithful and just and will forgive
us our sins and purify us from all unrighteous-
ness.*   1 John 1:8-9

We may try to deceive our friends or try to
hide our secret sins from our loved ones. Pride
may keep us from admitting we have lost control
of our life. Help, hope, and God's forgiveness
come when we admit the truth about ourselves.

> **Admitting our failure is a giant
> step toward the light.**

*But if we walk in the light, as he is in the light,
we have fellowship with one another, and the
blood of Jesus, his Son, purifies us from all sin.*
1 John 1:7

Having to cut ourselves off from our loved
ones is part of the price we pay for a secret life
of sin. One of the good gifts God returns to us
when we start the journey of recovery is the
good, clean feeling of not having to hide from
the ones we love—those who have been missing
our love and friendship.

> **God knows us; our failure didn't
> take him by surprise.**

*My little children, I am telling you this so that
you will stay away from sin. But if you sin, there
is someone to plead for you before the Father.
His name is Jesus Christ, the one who is all that
is good and who pleases God completely. He is
the one who took God's wrath against our sins
upon himself and brought us into fellowship with
God; and he is the forgiveness for our sins, and
not only ours but all the world's.*

1 John 2:1-2; TLB

If we thought we were perfect—or ever *could*
be in this life—we certainly know now that we
were wrong. God certainly knew it, which
explains why he made provision for our forgiveness. God wants us to desire to be like him.
When we fail along the way, he says, in effect,
"Get up; clean yourself up; and let's get going
again."

> **Remorse goes nowhere; true repentance leads to recovery.**

This then is . . . how we set our hearts at rest in his presence whenever our hearts condemn us. For God is greater than our hearts, and he knows everything.   1 John 3:19-20

The conscience God put within us makes us feel bad when we make bad choices. The Holy Spirit does not intend that these bad feelings send us into depression, for that kind of remorse goes nowhere but downward. Such guilt feelings are intended to drive us toward a loving God, who can forgive and restore us to physical, emotional, and spiritual health.

> ## We don't depend on our character to receive God's mercy; we rely on his!

And the Lord said, "I will cause all my goodness to pass in front of you, and I will proclaim my name, the Lord, in your presence. I will have mercy on whom I will have mercy, and I will have compassion on whom I will have compassion."
Exodus 33:19

Our heavenly Father really does want us to show a family resemblance in the way we live. But his love for us is not measured in terms of how good we become, but according to how merciful he is. The sooner we learn that God's love for us is unconditional, the sooner we can enjoy his affection and comfort.

> When we become the object of
> evil enemies, God becomes our
> special friend and protector.

*He is the refuge of the poor and humble when
evildoers are oppressing them.*   Psalm 14:6; TLB

Those who commit themselves to doing God's
will should expect opposition. The evil one
doesn't give up on anyone whom he has formerly
held in his power. At the same time, we can
expect all of God's protection when we start saying no to all the evil influences that used to cause
us to fall.

> **A loving father never demands**
> **more of his children than**
> **they can do.**

As a father has compassion on his children, so
the Lord has compassion on those who fear him;
for he knows how we are formed, he remembers
that we are dust.   Psalm 103:13-14

"**D**addy, I can't do it," many of us used to say
when a task was set before us that we thought
was beyond our ability. A loving Father knows
us better than we know ourselves—our
strengths and weaknesses, what we can do and
what we can't. If he says we can do it, we can do
it!

> **God loves us—delights in us!**
> **Think of that!**

The Lord delights in those who fear him, who put their hope in his unfailing love. Psalm 147:11

Good parents know how to treat their children when they admit they have done wrong. Children of loving parents know also that even when it is necessary, the discipline will be tempered by their parents' love for them. A good, loving God takes delight in us at all times, especially when we admit our failures and ask for his forgiveness and strength to start over again.

> **God would not be true to himself
> if he didn't act in love toward us.**

*For my own name's sake I delay my wrath; for
the sake of my praise I hold it back from you, so
as not to cut you off.*　　　　　Isaiah 48:9

All of us have sinned, and if justice were
done, all of us would be destroyed. But God
made the choice to send his Son, Jesus Christ,
to earth. Christ's death satisfied God's sense of
justice. Nothing we can ever do would make us
worthy of such love. We have committed our life
to a God who is committed to preserving his
people.

> The discipline of a loving father sometimes looks like anger—but there is love behind every stroke.

Foreigners will rebuild your walls, and their kings will serve you. Though in anger I struck you, in favor I will show you compassion.

Isaiah 60:10

Many of us have been hurting for a long time. We must realize that the hurting won't stop until we start making good choices again. When we turn our life over to God and seek his forgiveness, the pain can end. When it does, we will understand more than ever how God's hand of punishment can become a hand reaching out to comfort and strengthen us when the lesson is learned.

> **Because God loved us,
> he adopted us; he calls us
> his very own!**

*I will plant her for myself in the land; I will show
my love to the one I called "Not my loved one.
" I will say to those called "Not my people,"
"You are my people"; and they will say, "You
are my God."* Hosea 2:23

When we turned our life over to God, we
entered his family. Before we were strangers—
like orphans or homeless beggars, powerless and
hopeless. Now, as his children, we have available to us all of his power and protection. Knowing we have such a loving Father is a strong
incentive to want to please him and to act like
God's children.

God's gentle discipline today
keeps us from severe judgment
in the future.

---

*Oh, that he would make you truly see yourself,
for he knows everything you've done. Listen!
God is doubtless punishing you far less than you
deserve!*   Job 11:6; TLB

Prison and punishment are what criminals
deserve. Discipline, correction, and encouragement are what children receive who are loved by
their fathers. We may think God is being very
hard on us, but we can be thankful that he is a
merciful God, acting toward us not as a judge,
but as a loving father who wants to help us and
make us better.

> **God has already put away**
> **your sins, so put away**
> **your guilt feelings.**

He has removed our sins as far away from us as the east is from the west.   Psalm 103:12; TLB

As long as we struggle with guilt feelings, we will never feel free to move on toward better things and a better way of life. When we ask God's forgiveness, he takes away the guilt. We know that in our head, but sometimes our heart still can't let go of the guilt feelings. We need to take God at his word and start celebrating the fact that our sins no longer stand between us and our loving Father.

> **God knows everything; but he
> said he has forgotten your sins.**

I, even I, am he who blots out your transgressions, for my own sake, and remembers your sins no more.   Isaiah 43:25

It is one thing to know, as an objective fact, that our sins have been removed from the record books of heaven. It is another thing, much more comforting, to hear these words come from God himself. When we ask God to remove our sins and our shortcomings, we have this promise from him that he will do it.

> **God's forgiveness makes us
> his friends again.**

*"No longer will a man teach his neighbor, or a
man his brother, saying, 'Know the Lord,'
because they will all know me, from the least of
them to the greatest," declares the Lord. "For I
will forgive their wickedness and will remember
their sins no more."*   Jeremiah 31:34

We never really know how good our friends
are until we see just how much they are willing
to forgive us. Sometimes when we have offended
someone we love, they tell us we are forgiven,
but somehow things are never the same between
us again. God says that when he forgives, he forgets, so that we can be forever friends with him.

> **We can start out new—
> with a clean slate.**

*Therefore, if anyone is in Christ, he is a new
creation; the old has gone, the new has come!*
2 Corinthians 5:17

There is an enormous difference between a second chance and a new start! Turning over a new leaf, as we call it, is what we did many times in the past, but nothing happened. Once we turn our will and life over to God, he promises to make us new, with a new spirit, new life, and new strength to live as God intended.

> **Forgiving means forgetting—
> God said so!**

*For I will forgive their wickedness and will
remember their sins no more.*   Hebrews 8:12

Being forgiven by God doesn't give us an
excuse to forget the wrongs we did to others.
God forgave us so that we could start again, and
part of the new start is making a list of all those
we have harmed and being willing to make
amends to them all.

> **He forgave us for Jesus' sake.**

I write to you, dear children, because your sins have been forgiven on account of his name.
1 John 2:12

In accepting God's forgiveness, we must never forget the basis on which God was able to show us mercy. Our clean record before God is a result of what God's Son did for us by dying on the cross to remove the guilt of our sins. Living to please God now, accepting his help and strength to stay free from sinful bondage, is the best way to show him how much we appreciate what Jesus did for us.

> ### All the Father asks is "Come home, child!"

The Lord your God is gracious and compassionate. He will not turn his face from you if you return to him.   2 Chronicles 30:9

Sooner or later we lose patience and give up on people. But not God—he never gives up on us. No matter how far we stray, he is always willing to say, "Come home. Let me help you. Just turn around and come home."

Now God can comfort you.

The Lord will surely comfort Zion and will look with compassion on all her ruins; he will make her deserts like Eden, her wastelands like the garden of the Lord. Joy and gladness will be found in her, thanksgiving and the sound of singing.
                                                  Isaiah 51:3

Many parts of our past may seem beyond hope of recovery or restoration. As we look back, our life may resemble the smoking ruins of a building—the debris of wasted resources and a broken heart and spirit. We learn many things through these losses; but there is always the hope that some of those ruins can be rebuilt as we turn our life over to God.

> **You no longer have to be
> afraid of him.**

*Even though I walk through the valley of the
shadow of death, I will fear no evil, for you are
with me; your rod and your staff, they comfort
me.*   Psalm 23:4

The greatest enemy within us is not our weakness, but our fear. God's Spirit came in us to displace the spirit of fearfulness. With God as our
Shepherd and Protector, we have nothing to
fear; there are no enemies or temptations besetting us that we can't face with God at our side.

Discipline doesn't last forever.

My comfort in my suffering is this: Your promise preserves my life.   Psalm 119:50

Most of the pain we suffer is brought on by our own sin and rebellion. Sometimes we do suffer from others' wrongdoings, and at other times the pain results from our stand for God and what is right. Whatever the reason, God is our strength. If we suffer for righteousness, he will help us; if the suffering is discipline from his hand, we can be sure the pain will stop and his comfort will come when the lesson is learned.

> His discipline hurts, but it never
> comes without reason,
> and his comfort more than
> makes up for it.

Comfort, comfort my people, says your God.
Speak tenderly to Jerusalem, and proclaim to
her that her hard service has been completed,
that her sin has been paid for, that she has
received from the Lord's hand double for all her
sins. Isaiah 40:1-2

God always looks at discipline from the other
side; he seems as concerned as we are that the
lessons be learned so the punishment can end.
His purpose in it all is to bring us back to him.
When we have learned the lesson, he is quick to
apply the soothing balm of comfort and healing.

> **God is the special friend of the brokenhearted.**

*The Spirit of the Sovereign Lord is on me,
because the Lord has anointed me to preach
good news to the poor. He has sent me to bind up
the brokenhearted, to proclaim freedom for the
captives and release from darkness for the prisoners, to proclaim the year of the Lord's favor.*
                                        Isaiah 61:1-2

Those who grope for God in the darkness of
pain and bondage are the first to find him. The
self-sufficient, who think they can solve all their
own problems, never know the one who came to
give us hope and to set us free from the pain of a
broken heart, from the captivity of sin, and
from the sense of hopelessness sin brought on us.

> ## God says, "Stop crying, my child.
> ## It's forgiven now."

I will comfort you there as a little one is comforted by its mother. Isaiah 66:13; TLB

The world inflicts many kinds of pain on us. Pride sometimes keeps us from accepting God as an affectionate parent, who wants to hold us close and comfort us. When we turn our life and will over to him, we can count on his presence, his strength, and his solace.

**Sadness today—
gladness tomorrow.**

*Then maidens will dance and be glad, young
men and old as well. I will turn their mourning
into gladness; I will give them comfort and joy
instead of sorrow.* Jeremiah 31:13

Darkness has a way of magnifying sadness and
pain. The hope God promises for tomorrow is
harder to accept, but we must take God at his
word. As we keep our heart in touch with him
through prayer and meditation on his Word, the
message of hope will be there for us to reach out
and take.

> **Much good will result from
> all that pain.**

*Praise be to the God and Father of our Lord
Jesus Christ, the Father of compassion and the
God of all comfort, who comforts us in all our
troubles, so that we can comfort those in any
trouble with the comfort we ourselves have
received from God.*　　　2 Corinthians 1:3-4

Pain can be *sanctified*—"set apart for
a higher purpose." Just as with physical disease,
when healing for our spiritual illness occurs, a
kind of spiritual antibody called "God's comfort" stays in our system, available to apply to
others who suffer from the same kinds of sins
that nearly destroyed us. We must realize that
when healing finally comes to us, we will be able
to minister God's comfort to others who suffer
as we did.

Part Two

Dealing with the Past

*Put on the new man which
was created according to
God, in righteousness and
true holiness.* Ephesians 4:24; NKJV

> **God's help comes when we make
> a commitment to change.**

*If you put away the sin that is in your hand and
allow no evil to dwell in your tent, then you will
lift up your face without shame; you will stand
firm and without fear.*   Job 11:14-15

He is a gracious God, willing to forgive and
restore us. Yet he does not take any sin away
from us that we don't choose to give up. Peace
and joy come, as well as self-respect, when we
begin saying no to the things that controlled us
in the past.

> **God is always willing to help us
> when we want help.**

*O my rebellious children, come back to me again
and I will heal you from your sins.*

Jeremiah 3:22; TLB

Old destructive habits don't lose their hold on
us overnight. Saying no to temptation is a struggle we no longer have to face alone. God promises to help us, but we must want the help.

> **God loves unconditionally;
> recovery, however, is conditional.**

---

*I gave them this command: Obey me, and I will
be your God and you will be my people. Walk in
all the ways I command you, that it may go well
with you.*
Jeremiah 7:23

God doesn't ask anything from us that isn't
for our own good. His demanding strict obedience may sound harsh, but it is not nearly as
harsh as the consequences of not walking in his
ways. God really does want your life to go well—
today and every day.

> **God forgets our past if we
> commit our life to him.**

*But if a wicked man turns away from all the sins
he has committed and keeps all my decrees and
does what is just and right, he will surely live; he
will not die. None of the offenses he has committed will be remembered against him. Because of
the righteous things he has done, he will live.*

Ezekiel 18:21-22

Others say they forgive us, but they rarely
seem to forget. We may feel we are on probation
for a long time, and all eyes seem to be on us to
see how quickly we fail again. Not so with God!
He promises that if we turn back to him, he not
only forgives, but also forgets. His promise is the
one that counts.

❦

> **God is always there to meet us**
> **when we come back to him.**

Return, O Israel, to the Lord your God. Your sins have been your downfall! Take words with you and return to the Lord. Say to him: "Forgive all our sins and receive us graciously, that we may offer the fruit of our lips. . . ." [God's reply:] "I will heal their waywardness and love them freely, for my anger has turned away from them."   Hosea 14:1-2, 4

Sooner or later, the patience of all our friends and loved ones seems to run out. But God is always ready to accept us when we make the decision to turn our will and life over to his care.

**Pride keeps us from admitting
our powerlessness; meekness
opens the door for God's blessing.**

---

*Walk humbly and do what is right; perhaps even
yet the Lord will protect you from his wrath in
that day of doom.*   Zephaniah 2:3; TLB

Meekness is often interpreted today as weakness—but not in God's sight. Meekness really means strength under control. Admitting our needs is a wise, responsible act—a show of strength. It is also the way we make ourselves candidates for God's best.

**Confessing to God that we are
sinners is telling him what he
already knows.**

*But the tax collector stood at a distance. He
would not even look up to heaven, but beat his
breast and said, "God, have mercy on me, a sin-
ner." I tell you that this man, rather than the
other, went home justified before God. For everyone who exalts himself will be humbled, and he
who humbles himself will be exalted.*

Luke 18:13-14

These are days of looking for scapegoats—
someone in our past to blame for all the things
we do wrong. Until we accept responsibility for
our failures, we will never, like the tax collector,
"[go] home justified before God."

> ### Someone said, "Failure is an event—not a person."

When you are about to go into battle, the priest shall come forward and address the army. He shall say: "Hear, O Israel, today you are going into battle against your enemies. Do not be faint-hearted or afraid; do not be terrified or give way to panic before them. For the Lord your God is the one who goes with you to fight for you against your enemies to give you victory."

Deuteronomy 20:2-4

Humanly speaking, we have every reason to fear going out into the world, especially when we have failed over and over again when temptation struck. But this time it can be different. Today we may invite God to go with us. God's Word for today is: "Don't be fainthearted or afraid."

> As we walk in the light and in
> God's strength, we won't fail.

*The Lord is my light and my salvation—whom
shall I fear? The Lord is the stronghold of my
life—of whom shall I be afraid? When evil men
advance against me to devour my flesh, when
my enemies and my foes attack me, they will
stumble and fall. Though an army besiege me,
my heart will not fear; though war break out
against me, even then will I be confident.*

Psalm 27:1-3

We all tend to fear the unknown. Nothing
about the future can give us reason to be afraid,
since the Lord's guidance and strength make
safe our journey through today.

> The difference between crisis and
> calm is God's presence.

*God is our refuge and strength, an ever-present
help in trouble. Therefore we will not fear,
though the earth give way and the mountains
fall into the heart of the sea.*　　　Psalm 46:1-2

Some of those major surprises in life make us
panic and shrink away in fear and unbelief. A
steady, consistent seeking of God's presence
through prayer and meditation on his Word
provides the stability we need for such times.
With God at our side, the raging storm holds no
fear for us.

**With God watching over us, we
need not fear—or fail!**

*He will not let your foot slip—he who watches
over you will not slumber; indeed, he who
watches over Israel will neither slumber nor
sleep. The Lord watches over you—the Lord is
your shade at your right hand; the sun will not
harm you by day, nor the moon by night. The
Lord will keep you from all harm—he will watch
over your life.*   Psalm 121:3-7

Fearful people don't take risks, step out in
faith, or go on the offense against the evil in the
world. Our security is God himself. His eye on
us is all the protection and security we will ever
need.

> **Secure in our relationship with God, we aren't afraid of the forces of evil—both habits and people—that used to control us.**

Have no fear of sudden disaster or of the ruin that overtakes the wicked, for the Lord will be your confidence and will keep your foot from being snared.　　　　　Proverbs 3:25-26

Once we have turned our life over to God, asking him to take control of our will, we have made the best possible choice that could lead to our full recovery. God wants us to remember our enemies and how they gained control over us, lest we make the same mistakes again. But because we are now under God's protection, we don't fear them as we once did. We must count on God's promise to keep us today.

**Every day, give God the glory
for your victory.**

On the day the Lord gives you relief from suffering and turmoil and cruel bondage, you will take up this taunt against the king of Babylon: How the oppressor has come to an end! How his fury has ended!   Isaiah 14:3-4

When God gives us victory and then tells us to boast about it, we don't have to worry about it being real. Telling others the good news about what God has done for us not only reinforces in our own mind the truth, but it also encourages others to seek the same help from God that we have found.

> **Afraid of failure? Try to remember how many times God said in his Word, "Don't be afraid!" or "Fear not."**

Do not fear, for I am with you; do not be dismayed, for I am your God. I will strengthen you and help you; I will uphold you with my righteous right hand.   Isaiah 41:10

Before we allowed God to take control of our life, we had every reason to be afraid—that our commitment wouldn't stand, that temptation would once again become too strong to resist, or that old friends would drag us away again. Now that we are on God's side, he promises that he is with us to strengthen and help us. That is a promise we can trust.

**Staying close to God in prayer
is the best insurance against
failing again.**

---

*For the eyes of the Lord are on the righteous and
his ears are attentive to their prayer, but the
face of the Lord is against those who do evil.*

1 Peter 3:12

God loves us and wants us to stay close to him
in prayer. One benefit of prayer is that it keeps
us focused on the truth of God's love and how
much he wants us to call on him when we need
help to stand against temptation.

> **God wants us to begin right**
> **now to commit ourselves**
> **completely to his care.**

When you lie down, you will not be afraid; when
you lie down, your sleep will be sweet.

Proverbs 3:24

Many times we go through an entire day trying to face the world all by ourselves. Then we
go to bed at night and worry about all we did
wrong, fearful that tomorrow will be no better.
God promises us that if we turn our cares over
to him and let him do for us what we can't do for
ourselves, we will enjoy not only a good night's
sleep, but a restful tomorrow.

> **How bright is the future? As bright as the promises of God!**

He will swallow up death forever. The Sovereign Lord will wipe away the tears from all faces; he will remove the disgrace of his people from all the earth. The Lord has spoken.

Isaiah 25:8

Yesterday may have been a sad experience of defeat and discouragement. But God wants to change all that and begin the transformation right now. When we make the decision to turn our life and will over to him, loving Father that he is, he takes over. He promises to dry our tears and help us change so that tomorrow can be a day of victory and joy.

> ### The safest place to be is where God is.

But now, this is what the Lord says—he who created you, O Jacob, he who formed you, O Israel: "Fear not, for I have redeemed you; I have summoned you by name; you are mine. When you pass through the waters, I will be with you; and when you pass through the rivers, they will not sweep over you. When you walk through the fire, you will not be burned; the flames will not set you ablaze."
Isaiah 43:1-2

True, today and tomorrow may be filled with trouble. But we must never forget who promised to go with us to comfort, encourage, strengthen, and protect us.

> **Tomorrow will dawn bright and clear; God said so.**

In righteousness you will be established: Tyranny will be far from you; you will have nothing to fear. Terror will be far removed; it will not come near you.   Isaiah 54:14

Peace isn't being in a place of quiet tranquility— nor in a comfortable spot on a peaceful, calm, spring day. Peace is being held close and safe by a loving God while a terrible storm is crashing all around us. We face tomorrow knowing that God has committed himself to our care and protection.

> **The opposite of faith isn't
> doubt—it is fear!**

*He said to his disciples, "Why are you so afraid?
Do you still have no faith?"*   Mark 4:40

When we place our confidence in Christ, we
have every reason to believe that he commits
himself to taking care of us. We may suffer hard
times, but even then we know God is with us and
is working out even our pain for our good and
his glory. Being afraid is an indication that we
don't really think God can keep his promises.
He can! He will!

> **The Shepherd is also a king.**
> **Someday we will reign with him.**

Do not be afraid, little flock, for your Father
has been pleased to give you the kingdom.

Luke 12:32

Many say that sheep are among the most
helpless domesticated animals. Without a shepherd they have no future. But our Shepherd
says that he knows how to care for those who
have committed themselves to him. Each morning the sheep go out with a trustworthy shepherd, and they all return safely to the fold each
night. Tomorrow will be the same for us as long
as Christ is our Shepherd.

> **We can be fearless today,**
> **tomorrow, and forever.**

No, in all these things we are more than conquerors through him who loved us. For I am convinced that neither death nor life, neither angels nor demons, neither the present nor the future, nor any powers, neither height nor depth, nor anything else in all creation, will be able to separate us from the love of God that is in Christ Jesus our Lord.   Romans 8:37-39

Almost every dimension and condition, human and spiritual, is mentioned in this promise of God. We have no fear—because the one who made this promise is Almighty God, and because we can never be separated from his love.

❦

> **We stay in bondage of soul until
> we are certain that we are
> forgiven.**

*For I admit my shameful deed—it haunts me
day and night. It is against you and you alone I
sinned and did this terrible thing. Sprinkle me
with cleansing blood and I shall be clean again.*
                              Psalm 51:3-4, 7; TLB

When we admit that we are unable to control
our life because of our sinful nature and habits,
God stands ready to grant us forgiveness when
we ask it of him. God knows that we need to feel
released from the burden of guilt. And he has
provided the means. Guilt feelings can go away
when we are convinced that he has removed the
guilt that caused the feelings.

> We can hold our head up high
> again, because a forgiving God
> has taken away our shame.

Do not be afraid; you will not suffer shame. Do not fear disgrace; you will not be humiliated. You will forget the shame of your youth and remember no more the reproach of your widowhood.
Isaiah 54:4

Sin and its entrapments spoiled our record before God as they defiled our soul and body. God's forgiveness removes the sinful record. His grace through Christ's sacrifice on our behalf also provided a means of cleansing, so that the reasons we felt ashamed are removed. If a pure and holy God can forgive us, certainly people like us, who are just as subject to sin as we are, should be able to forgive us as well.

> ### God makes us an offer we can—but shouldn't—refuse.

"Come now, let us reason together," says the Lord. "Though your sins are like scarlet, they shall be as white as snow; though they are red as crimson, they shall be like wool."

Isaiah 1:18

Our Creator takes no pleasure in punishing sin. His heart of love would prefer that we allow him to do what needs to be done to make us acceptable to him and the holiness of heaven. This kind of cleansing and forgiveness can take place the moment we turn our life over to him. He is always ready to forgive those sins we fall into as we go through life. "Come," God says.

❧

> **God forgives and frees us—so we
> can be free to forgive.**

*Therefore, there is now no condemnation for
those who are in Christ Jesus, because through
Christ Jesus the law of the Spirit of life set me
free from the law of sin and death.*

Romans 8:1-2

Those who can't forgive others—who hold
grudges against people who have hurt them—
are often themselves feeling unforgiven for some
wrongs they may have done. When Christ sets
us free, telling us that there is no longer any
record of sin being held against us, we should
feel compelled to go out and settle all of our old,
outstanding accounts, forgiving and being forgiven.

> **When Almighty God does anything, he does it perfectly.**

I, even I, am he who blots out your transgressions, for my own sake, and remembers your sins no more.   Isaiah 43:25

It is not some other frail, temperamental person who has forgiven us. It is God himself who has removed our sins. Such forgiveness is complete and leaves no place for guilt feelings. Feelings of gratitude? Yes, but not guilt feelings!

**The basis of our being
forgiven people is that we have
a *forgiving God.***

---

*Therefore, as God's chosen people, holy and
dearly loved, clothe yourselves with compassion,
kindness, humility, gentleness and patience. Bear
with each other and forgive whatever grievances
you may have against one another. Forgive as
the Lord forgave you.*

Colossians 3:12-13

Forgiveness does not come easy for some of us.
The reason is clearly explained here. We find it
hard to forgive because we haven't allowed God
to make us compassionate enough, kind enough,
humble enough, gentle enough, or patient
enough. As a benevolent father, he offers us, his
beloved children, this beautiful new wardrobe!
Today God can clothe us with all of these lovely
qualities if we allow him to do so. God never commands us to do what he won't provide the means
to accomplish. That is a promise!

> **God wants us to remember
> him as being compassionate
> and forgiving.**

You will again have compassion on us; you will tread our sins underfoot and hurl all our iniquities into the depths of the sea.   Micah 7:19

We all go through hard times—experiences that many of us deserve. Failure makes us want to shrink away and give up. God reminds us that he forgives all the sins we are willing to admit. If we turn our sins over to him, he knows a place to throw them so that they will never be found again!

> We not only have the best *example* of forgiveness—we have the most powerful *means* at our disposal: God's power.

Be merciful, just as your Father is merciful. Do not judge, and you will not be judged. Do not condemn, and you will not be condemned. Forgive, and you will be forgiven.

Luke 6:36-37

When we enter into risky situations, we often want someone else to go first. This verse sounds as if God won't forgive us until we forgive others. God is more gracious than we are; he forgives us based on his grace. But he has a lesson to teach us. If he can forgive us, we certainly should be able to forgive others.

Part Three

Thinking Straight

*And the peace of God,
which transcends all understanding, will guard your
hearts and your minds in
Christ Jesus.* **Philippians 4:7**

> **Our responsibility is to do our
> best right now; God will take
> care of the rest of the day.**

*The Lord himself goes before you and will be
with you; he will never leave you nor forsake
you. Do not be afraid; do not be discouraged.*
Deuteronomy 31:8

We all must admit that we spend too much
time fretting over the wasted past, feeling appre-
hensive, and expecting tomorrow to be more of
the same. God is the Lord of today, and he
wants us to live each moment of today to the full-
est. When we commit our life and will to him,
every moment can be an exciting, victorious, joyful adventure.

> **As long as we are prepared to do anything God says, we won't fall today.**

Though he stumble, he will not fall, for the Lord upholds him with his hand. Psalm 37:24

A tightrope walker never looks down at the rope on which he treads. His eye is always straight ahead, focused on the goal—the end of the rope ahead. God wants us to think about obeying him, walking the path he lays out for us. When we do our best in that area, God will take care of our safety. No one falls who is holding tightly to God's hand.

> **God wants us to step out in faith
> and stretch our comfort zone.**

*Therefore, prepare your minds for action; be
self-controlled; set your hope fully on the grace
to be given you when Jesus Christ is revealed.*

1 Peter 1:13

There is a balance we must strike between
being overcautious and presumptuously stepping out beyond what God asks us to do. God
expects us to move beyond our fearful inhibi-
tions and move out with him, even when we feel
we are beyond ourselves and our own abilities.
There is no limit to what God can do with any of
us today if we are willing to follow him through
the curtain of the unknown.

God knows our needs. Being
content with what he gives us
today proves we trust him.

*The name of the Lord is a strong tower; the
righteous run to it and are safe.*   Proverbs 18:10

When we are taking a moral inventory of
our life in order to make amends wherever
possible, we may think of many things that make
us fearful. To set some things right will arouse
old anger in those we have hurt. Our pride and
fear may tend to keep us from settling all these
accounts. But before God, we know it is the
right thing to do. He promises today to be our
strong tower. The safest place for anyone to be
is in the center of God's will.

❦

> **Yesterday was yesterday.**
> **Today—this moment right now—**
> **should have our full attention.**

Keep falsehood and lies far from me; give me neither poverty nor riches, but give me only my daily bread. Otherwise, I may have too much and disown you and say, "Who is the Lord?" Or I may become poor and steal, and so dishonor the name of my God.   Proverbs 30:8-9

Contentment is a state of mind—not a bank statement or health report. Discontent comes when we start the vicious cycle of self-pity, thinking God can't or won't provide for us—the thought pattern that got us into bondage in the first place. God's Word for us is that his supply for today is his careful and loving assessment of what is best for us right now.

> **If we can trust our soul to some-
> one while we are asleep, we can
> certainly trust our life to one
> who walks beside us all day long!**

*I will lie down and sleep in peace, for you alone,
O Lord, make me dwell in safety.*   Psalm 4:8

Sooner or later in our walk toward recovery
we must accept the truth that if God can't or
won't protect us, we are without hope. Since we
know that God's love does surround us, and
that he has committed himself to our protection,
we can be confident that recovery is not only
possible, but something God desires for us. We
need to address today's prospects and problems
with this refreshing promise from God in mind.

> **Today, more than we need
> food—and sleep—we need the
> confidence that God is
> taking care of us.**

*In vain you rise early and stay up late, toiling
for food to eat—for he grants sleep to those he
loves.*   Psalm 127:2

We spend much of our time with the details of
food, clothing, and shelter. Earthbound as we
are, we lose sight of the fact that an eternal God
has committed himself to watch over us. The
most and the best the world offers us means
nothing unless we can rest in the peace that
comes from knowing his love surrounds us.

> Let us take God at his word
> today and step out,
> knowing he is with us.

Though I walk in the midst of trouble, you pre-serve my life; you stretch out your hand against the anger of my foes, with your right hand you save me. Psalm 138:7

The consequences of many of the problems we created during the past are still around today. God, in his goodness, sometimes removes the consequences, but often he doesn't. The fact that others cannot forgive us must not deter us from trying to live for God moment by moment, or cause us to give up in discouragement. We must leave with God what may result from the anger others still feel toward us. Our task for today is to do what we know is right and leave the consequences with a loving God.

> **The one who cares for all his creation sees us and knows our needs.**

The eyes of all look to you, and you give them their food at the proper time. You open your hand and satisfy the desires of every living thing.
                                        Psalm 145:15-16

The world of nature has much to teach us about God's care. Jesus also reminded us that the One who cares for the lilies of the field and the sparrows cares about us. Turning our life over to his care and keeping is a wise decision. Today is a good day to express to God our gratitude by accepting his power and guidance to walk in victory.

> God's standards are high;
> he expects good things from us,
> but nothing that he hasn't
> given us the strength and
> encouragement to do.

His divine power has given us everything we need for life and godliness through our knowledge of him who called us by his own glory and goodness.   2 Peter 1:3

We can't say recovery is impossible because of our lack of education or training, or because our parents didn't give us a proper upbringing. All of these limit the way we function in some areas of life, but God said that when we know his Son, Jesus Christ, we are given everything we need to live as he wants us to live.

> **Old temptations don't have the same grip on us when God takes control of our life.**

Free me from the trap that is set for me, for you are my refuge.　　　　Psalm 31:4

Since that moment when we committed our life and will to God, we have struggled with the old urges and temptations to return to the kind of life that nearly destroyed us. When we realized how powerless we were, we turned our life over to God, who is able to make us stand. The traps are still there, and the old desires still lurk within us—but God has promised us that as we walk with him, he will keep us from becoming ensnared again.

> **Victory comes by winning the
> battles one at a time.**

*You need to persevere so that when you have
done the will of God, you will receive what he
has promised.* Hebrews 10:36

The great suffering some of us have endured
has etched away our ability to endure pain.
Long-term pain does not necessarily make us
more able to endure suffering; in fact, sometimes we become more impatient because of it.
Today, while recovery is underway, we must be
patient and accept God's promise that he will
help us if we hold on to him.

❦

> **The disease of sin has taken its toll. God promises healing will come one day at a time.**

Then your light will break forth like the dawn, and your healing will quickly appear; then your righteousness will go before you, and the glory of the Lord will be your rear guard.   Isaiah 58:8

The Scriptures often compare sickness and sin. Sometimes one is used metaphorically of the other. Both require healing—one of the body, the other of the soul and spirit. Body and soul, we daily need God's healing touch. One day he will take all the mystery out of our suffering and pain, but until then, we must commit ourselves to following the light he gives us.

❧

> **God said we are safe with him.**
> **Because he said it, it is true.**
> **Then he swore by himself that it**
> **was true. What could be more**
> **true than God's double oath!**

God did this so that, by two unchangeable things
in which it is impossible for God to lie, we who
have fled to take hold of the hope offered to us
may be greatly encouraged. We have this hope
as an anchor for the soul, firm and secure. It
enters the inner sanctuary behind the curtain.
Hebrews 6:18-19

The veil in the temple, around which the
nation of Israel worshipped, represented the sep-
aration between God and man. When Jesus died
on the cross, this veil in the temple was literally
torn in two, giving us direct access to our heavenly Father. The most safeguarded declarations
in the universe are God's promises; the most
dependable being is God himself; and the most
secure place is where God is, and we are there!

> Nothing can happen to us today
> that can penetrate God's
> protective wall set around us.

He will cover you with his feathers, and under his wings you will find refuge; his faithfulness will be your shield and rampart. You will not fear the terror of night, nor the arrow that flies by day, nor the pestilence that stalks in the darkness, nor the plague that destroys at midday.

Psalm 91:4-6

Struggling with the sins that took control of us has filled us with fear. Getting free meant saying no to many things, which spread a pall of negativism over us. But that night of terror is over now that God has taken us under his protective care. He wants us to forget yesterday and approach life today on a positive note. His promise of protection rests on us.

God's timing is perfect.
He heard us when we first
prayed, and he will answer at
exactly the right time.

*I waited patiently for the Lord; he turned to me
and hear my cry.* Psalm 40:1

Chronological time and psychological time
rarely seem the same. During long nights of suffering, it seems the dawn of joy and comfort will
never come. It is easier to be patient when we
realize that, when we feel most desperate, God is
there in the darkness with us, holding our hand.

> We usually learn more from pain
> than pleasure.

*We also rejoice in our sufferings, because we
know that suffering produces perseverance; perseverance, character; and character, hope.*
Romans 5:3-4

At these times, when people seem most concerned about health, wealth, beauty, and comfort, we are tempted to be caught up in the
world's warped values. Following God's ways
often leads through paths of suffering, sacrifice,
and personal loss. In the process God gives us
qualities far more valuable than good physical
or material fortune: perseverance, character,
and hope.

Patience doesn't come naturally;
it is a product of the
Spirit within us.

But the fruit of the Spirit is love, joy, peace,
patience.   Galatians 5:22

Some of us, as a result of good upbringing and
personal strength, develop some winsome character traits. But even when we are at our best,
we usually lack the right motivation for good
character and behavior. So that we may be all
that we can be—loving, joyful, peaceable, and
patient—God sent his Spirit to live in us to produce these qualities as choice fruit from a well-
nurtured tree.

> **God is patient, waiting for us to
> get better; we must also be
> patient with the process.**

*Bear in mind that our Lord's patience means sal-
vation, just as our dear brother Paul also wrote
you with the wisdom that God gave him.*
                                                    2 Peter 3:15

We should be thankful that God did not close
the books on us before we finally returned to
sane thinking and accepted what he wanted to
do to help us recover. We can be thankful for
God's patience in not taking us away to judgment. We need to be grateful to God for his goodness and patience. Without it we would have no
hope.

> **The end is in sight; the long wait
> has made us a better person.**

*You know that the testing of your faith develops
perseverance. Perseverance must finish its work
so that you may be mature and complete, not
lacking anything.*   James 1:3-4

God can change the record books about us
immediately, but it often takes time for God to
rebuild character in us. The process may be
long, slow, and painful. God's timing is perfect.
Our impatience with God will only sabotage the
final product. Today, we must allow him full control if we want the process to be done right.

> **Better days are coming. The question is not *if*, but *when*.**

Be patient, then, brothers, until the Lord's coming. See how the farmer waits for the land to yield its valuable crop and how patient he is for the autumn and spring rains. You too, be patient and stand firm, because the Lord's coming is near.   James 5:7-8

Those who till the soil have an advantage over people who have come to expect instant results. We must learn to take the long-range view about our recovery. As we seek to grow closer to God, we will learn more of what he is doing in our life and why. Knowing that the harvest of blessing is certain, we, like the farmer, can be confident and patient.

> **Anything good is worth
> waiting for.**

*But if we hope for what we do not yet have, we
wait for it patiently.*   Romans 8:25

Children anxiously awaiting the coming of
Christmas morning are joyful in their wait,
because they know with certainty that morning
will come. Knowing that God's promises to us
are true and the future is certain, we have every
reason to be as filled with joy as a child awaiting
Christmas morning.

> **As we return to a more sane way
> of life, God will help us restore
> our reputation.**

*No one whose hope is in you will ever be put to
shame, but they will be put to shame who are
treacherous without excuse.*   Psalm 25:3

A reputation that took a lifetime to build can
be destroyed or badly damaged in a moment.
Character is the quality God most wants to
develop. Character will stand the test of time.
As we turn our life over to God and do all we
can to make restitution for the wrongs we have
done, God will take care of how we appear to
others. He is our defense.

> **We learn even during the times
> of waiting, but someday God's
> promise of full restoration
> will become a reality.**

*We wait in hope for the Lord; he is our help and
our shield.*   Psalm 33:20

The world is filled with disappointments.
People will let us down. If we make other people
the foundation of our hope, we will soon become
disillusioned. But if our hope is fixed on God's
promise, we can be confident that the future
holds no dread for us.

> **Progress seems slow when hopes
> run high, but restoration will
> come as we keep our eyes on him.**

Why are you downcast, O my soul? Why so disturbed within me? Put your hope in God, for I will yet praise him, my Savior and my God.
Psalm 42:11

Sometimes we talk and think ourselves into a depressed state. Projecting in our minds the worst possible scenario is the surest way to get down emotionally. In this passage, the Psalmist shares his secret: we should talk ourselves out of depression instead of into it. The future based on hope in God is a sure hope.

> As we grow stronger,
> we can anticipate being able
> to help others.

There is surely a future hope for you, and your hope will not be cut off.　　　　Proverbs 23:18

A sentiment commonly expressed during the worst of our pain is the hope that we will some-day recover so we can warn others away from the danger spots into which we strayed. Sharing the good news about where we found strength to overcome will be a part of our recovery process, one of our joyful expectations—knowing that God can once again use us to help others.

> **We will grow stronger each
> day as we continue with God on
> the way to recovery.**

But for you who revere my name, the sun of righteousness will rise with healing in its wings. And you will go out and leap like calves released from the stall.   Malachi 4:2

The crippled man Jesus healed rose up and leaped for joy. Our spirit will also rejoice as we express our gratitude to God for restoring us to a life of freedom from the entrapments of our sinful past. Today we can enter into joy as we anticipate the completion of the healing that is now in progress.

3 / 27

> **One day we will experience full
> healing of body, soul, and spirit.**

*The faith and love that spring from the hope
that is stored up for you in heaven and that you
have already heard about in the word of truth,
the gospel.*   Colossians 1:5

Our hope for recovery is not built on some
nebulous idea of an impersonal power that we
may somehow find by groping around in the
dark. We have the certainty of God's clear revelation about the remedy for sin and its power
over us. Once we receive God on his terms, we
have access to the power of our all-powerful
Creator.

> **A living hope is one that never
> fades with time.**

*Praise be to the God and Father of our Lord
Jesus Christ! In his great mercy he has given us
new birth into a living hope through the resurrection of Jesus Christ from the dead, and into
an inheritance that can never perish, spoil or
fade—kept in heaven for you.* 1 Peter 1:3-4

We have the bright hope of an eternity with
God in heaven. But we don't have to wait until
heaven for the kingdom of God. It can rule in
our hearts even here on earth as we accept
God's power and sovereignty over us. Becoming
God's subjects, we also become his sons and
daughters and enter into all the privileges and
blessings of our Father's throne.

> **We aren't yet what we should be,
> but one day we will be!**

How great is the love the Father has lavished on us, that we should be called children of God! And that is what we are! The reason the world does not know us is that it did not know him. Dear friends, now we are children of God, and what we will be has not yet been made known. But we know that when he appears, we shall be like him, for we shall see him as he is. Everyone who has this hope in him purifies himself, just as he is pure. 1 John 3:1-3

Knowing God has removed from us the burden of a sinful past, and knowing we will one day be like our Lord Jesus in character and nature, we have the greatest incentive to want to be like him here and now.

Part Four

===

Keeping Close to God

*To them God has chosen to
make known among the Gen-
tiles the glorious riches of this
mystery, which is Christ in
you, the hope of glory.*

Colossians 1:27

> The formula for success, as God
> sees success, is clear—meditation
> on his Word and obedience
> to his commands.

*Do not let this Book of the Law depart from
your mouth; meditate on it day and night, so
that you may be careful to do everything written
in it. Then you will be prosperous and success-
ful.*   Joshua 1:8

Many times we don't understand why God
asks us in his Word to do certain things. Yet
behind every command is a purpose, a challenge, and a promise of his presence to help us
achieve all he expects of us. Today he will prove
to us how good he is if we allow him to rule in
our life.

> **God will give us direction for tomorrow as we walk in the light he gives today.**

For these commands are a lamp, this teaching is a light, and the corrections of discipline are the way to life. Proverbs 6:23

The world around us claimed to have the answers to our problems. Some of these "answers" led us into the prison of entrapment, and now we struggle daily to regain control of our life. When we committed ourselves to God for his control, he offered us a clear way to health and hope. As we meditate today on his Word, we have all the light, direction, and correction that we need for freedom from sin's power.

> **The more we meditate on
> God's promises, the more faith
> we have to face today.**

Consequently, faith comes from hearing the message, and the message is heard through the word of Christ.   Romans 10:17

Faith does not come from trying to pump up our sense of self-trust. The world says, "Believe in yourself!" but we know now that our only real foundation of faith is in what Christ promised in his Word. Believing that he is with us today as we abide in his Word can be the difference between finding strength and encouragement or sliding again into defeat.

> **No person is really wise who
> hasn't grounded his faith in
> God's Word.**

From infancy you have known the holy Scriptures, which are able to make you wise for salvation through faith in Christ Jesus. All Scripture is God-breathed and is useful for teaching, rebuking, correcting and training in righteousness.   2 Timothy 3:15-16

What can we really count on in today's changing world? Many philosophies promise us wisdom, inner strength, and stability. We have tried some and discovered just how unhelpful they were. The only sure foundation is what God has given us in "the holy Scriptures" to make us wise, to teach, instruct, and to keep us under control. Meditating on God's Word gives us all the wisdom we need for today.

> **Growth is a certainty if
> our source of nourishment is
> what it should be.**

*Like newborn babies, crave pure spiritual milk,
so that by it you may grow up in your salvation.*
1 Peter 2:2

Babies can't take strong food; their nourishment is assimilated first through the mother's body. But the day comes when the child, well nourished on milk, will be able to stand on his own. Though we may temporarily depend on others, our need for the nourishment of the Word of God will never be outgrown. If we want to prosper today, we need to meditate on the Word of God to receive what he wants to give us.

> **Our life and our relationship
> to God depends on the life-
> giving Word of God.**

I am not ashamed of the gospel, because it is the power of God for the salvation of everyone who believes.
Romans 1:16

Through prayer and meditation on the Scriptures we learned how important our relationship to God is. Our connection to all of God's strength and help is through that relationship. Everything we accomplish today that is of lasting value will be the result of our walking in the light of God's Word.

> **The first rule of good building is
> to develop a solid foundation.**

*Heaven and earth will pass away, but my words
will never pass away.* Matthew 24:35

All our wealth and strength will be gone some-
day. All that this world offers is transient. Our
only foundation for the future and today is God
and his Word to us. In all our efforts today, we
need to remember that it is only as our will con-
forms to God's will that we can have any stability. His promises of help are trustworthy
because his Word will never pass away.

It is one thing to know
God's Word; what really counts is
that we act out our trust
in it day by day.

*Blessed is the one who reads the words of this
prophecy, and blessed are those who hear it and
take to heart what is written in it, because the
time is near.* Revelation 1:3

Without prayer to our heavenly Father and
meditation on his Word, we have no guidance on
the path. Temptations still come, and we are
weak and unwise. Only God's strength and wisdom will make today a day of victory.

> **The world around is noisy; only a heart tuned to God hears him.**

Listen to me, O house of Jacob, all you who remain of the house of Israel, you whom I have upheld since you were conceived, and have carried since your birth.   Isaiah 46:3

The one who has created and redeemed us asks us to sit quietly and listen. When we lose sight of God as Creator and Sustainer, his voice grows faint—not because he isn't speaking, but because, like sheep, we drift away too far to hear the shepherd's voice. He has promised to continue to sustain us. Today we must stay in range of his voice to enjoy his peace and safety.

> **There's a feast underway, and you and I are invited!**

Come, all you who are thirsty, come to the waters; and you who have no money, come, buy and eat! Come, buy wine and milk without money and without cost. Why spend money on what is not bread, and your labor on what does not satisfy? Listen, listen to me, and eat what is good, and your soul will delight in the richest of fare. Isaiah 55:1-2

One of the most thrilling invitations in Scripture is made here by the Creator God to his people. He asks us to turn from all the things that we thought would satisfy us, but didn't. Today, the feast is prepared for us. When we turn our life and will over to God, we enter the banquet room with him. Just come!

> The place of safety today is
> within range of the Good
> Shepherd's voice.

*My sheep listen to my voice; I know them, and
they follow me. I give them eternal life, and they
shall never perish; no one can snatch them out
of my hand.*   John 10:27-28

Many strange voices call us each day. Before
we turned our life and will over to God's care,
some of these voices sounded attractive. Now
that we understand God's will, we can tell the
difference. Those who stay near to the Shepherd
have the promise from him that they will never
perish.

> **Meditating on God's Word
> gives us light and wisdom to
> know the truth.**

*We know that Christ, God's Son, has come to
help us understand and find the true God. And
now we are in God because we are in Jesus
Christ his Son, who is the only true God; and he
is eternal Life.*   1 John 5:20; TLB

Now that we understand that we are under his
care, we also recognize that he not only walks
with us but, by his Spirit, he is in us, living the
life of Christ through us. Our relationship to
God is secure forever; how much more secure
are we today as we stand against temptation!

> The wise person is one who is
> simple enough to accept God's
> Word as light and truth.

*The unfolding of your words gives light; it gives
understanding to the simple.*   Psalm 119:130

Some try to make our relationship to God a
very complicated thing. God used simple terms
to explain our relationship; we are sheep to a
Good Shepherd; children to a loving Father. His
Word is called a lamp that gives light. Today let
us in simple trust accept God's Word as words of
a loving Father, and the truths of his Word as
light upon a dark path to keep us from stum-
bling.

> **God has put a strong link between right knowledge and right actions.**

Anyone who listens to the word but does not do what it says is like a man who looks at his face in a mirror and, after looking at himself, goes away and immediately forgets what he looks like. But the man who looks intently into the perfect law that gives freedom, and continues to do this, not forgetting what he has heard, but doing it—he will be blessed in what he does.

James 1:23-25

The proof that we know and believe God's Word is when we take it to be true and act on it. The way to happiness, peace, and power to stand against temptation is to live out the truth as we know it moment by moment.

> **God's Word is his love letter
> to us—messages from
> his heart to ours.**

*Your words are what sustain me; they are food
to my hungry soul. They bring joy to my sorrow-
ing heart and delight me. How proud I am to
bear your name, O Lord.*   Jeremiah 15:16; TLB

Now that we have placed our trust in what
God has done for us through Jesus Christ, we
have a new relationship with him. Once we take
on his name, not only will our attitude toward
him change, but so will our attitude toward
other attractions. The more we come to treasure
God's Word, the revelation of his love for us,
the less attractive other objects become to us.

> **He knows us by name; his call to
> us means he is going ahead,
> preparing the way for us.**

*The sheep listen to his voice. He calls his own
sheep by name and leads them out. When he has
brought out all his own, he goes on ahead of
them, and his sheep follow him because they
know his voice.* John 10:3-4

A good shepherd doesn't stand behind his
flock, thrashing at them to keep them moving.
His sheep know that to follow his voice is to walk
in safe paths to good feeding grounds. Meditating on God's Word and listening to his voice
today will lead us to safe, pleasant places.

> **Trust in God, delight in him,
> and you will live and enjoy
> safe pastures.**

Trust in the Lord and do good; dwell in the land and enjoy safe pasture. Delight yourself in the Lord and he will give you the desires of your heart. Commit your way to the Lord; trust in him.
Psalm 37:3-5

All through the Scriptures we are pictured as being God's sheep. Without the Shepherd we would be lost. Living close to him means safety and the provision of all our needs. Only those who seek their satisfaction elsewhere end up in disaster. Today, we can enjoy all the blessings of God's sheepfold. All we need to do is listen to his voice and follow.

4 / 17

> Following God's voice some-
> times puts us on a lonely path.
> Yet it is the only way that leads to
> help and hope.

Blessed is the man who makes the Lord his trust,
who does not look to the proud, to those who
turn aside to false gods.   Psalm 40:4

When everyone is turning to hear this person's or that person's voice, it is hard for us to
stand alone and choose to listen only to what
God is saying. Too much of our past was ruined
by listening to the wrong voices. Today, the way
of safety is the path God is calling us to follow.

> When we see how powerless we
> are, the more we need the solid
> foundation of trust in God.

*Those who trust in the Lord are like Mount
Zion, which cannot be shaken but endures
forever.*   Psalm 125:1

The center of the world to God's people,
Israel, was Zion, the mountain on which the
temple was built. The temple, the place where
God made his presence known, was considered
to be their foundation for national and religious
security. A more firm foundation than Zion is
ours today as we turn our life and will over to
God.

> We either trust in God or trust
> in ourselves; only our trust
> in God promises a good journey
> on a straight path.

*Trust in the Lord with all your heart and lean
not on your own understanding; in all your ways
acknowledge him, and he will make your paths
straight.* Proverbs 3:5-6

We often begin by saying we are trusting in God. Then, at the least feeling of insecurity, we tend to try again to take over the control of our life. The results of such an action proves, each time we do so, that God's way is best. Today, God offers us a promise of a safe trip through dangerous country. Our responsibility is to trust him—not ourselves.

> **The difference between being
> a fool and a wise man depends on
> whose wisdom we are trusting—
> ours or God's.**

*He who trusts in the Lord will prosper. He who
trusts in himself is a fool, but he who walks in
wisdom is kept safe.*   Proverbs 28:25-26

It is true that God gave us good minds, and
many decisions we make every day are decisions
God intends for us to make. Yet there are times
when we know that we need to look beyond ourselves for help and strength. It was our self-trust
that put us under the control of sin. It was a
wise decision for us to turn our life and will over
to God. Today, we must keep making the wise
decision to trust God and not ourselves.

> **God's word for us today is,
> "Do not worry!"**

*So do not worry, saying, "What shall we eat?"
or "What shall we drink?" or "What shall we
wear?" For the pagans run after all these
things, and your heavenly Father knows that
you need them. But seek first his kingdom and
his righteousness, and all these things will be
given to you as well.*   Matthew 6:31-33

Most of the things we fear will happen, never
do happen. Too much of our valuable time,
which should be spent in worthwhile work for
God, gets used up in our search for the things
God said he would provide. Today let us get our
priorities straight and concern ourselves with
seeking God and his kingdom. He can take care
of us.

> There is no point in getting
> worried about details about
> which God said he would oversee.

*Let him have all your worries and cares, for he
is always thinking about you and watching
everything that concerns you.*

1 Peter 5:7; TLB

We say that we care *about* someone we love.
God says he cares *for* us, meaning he is watching
over us as a shepherd watches his sheep. God
does love us, but because he does, he wants the
very best for us. When we turn our life over to
his control, we can be sure that he will do what
is best. Today, we must stop worrying and start
trusting.

> **God speaks through his Word;**
> **now he waits to hear ours.**

The Lord is near to all who call on him, to all who call on him in truth. He fulfills the desires of those who fear him; he hears their cry and saves them. Psalm 145:18-19

During a hard, busy day, it is easy to forget *who* we are and *whose* we are. The Lord is very near, available to hear us at any moment. Dark day or bright, in heaviness or happiness, he wants us to call out to him.

> **Sometimes it is hard to get others' attention when we need help; but God's ear is always open to hear us.**

Then you will call upon me and come and pray to me, and I will listen to you. You will seek me and find me when you seek me with all your heart. Jeremiah 29:12-13

God doesn't like halfhearted people. He once said that lukewarm people make him sick. He wants us to be bold as we seek to learn about him in prayer and meditation on his Word. Today, as we seek God with all our heart, he will hear and answer. We need him; today we need to stay on speaking terms with him.

> Those who love God's Son are
> given special access to the Father.

*In that day you will no longer ask me anything.
I tell you the truth, my Father will give you
whatever you ask in my name. Until now you
have not asked for anything in my name. Ask
and you will receive, and your joy will be complete.*
John 16:23-24

Jesus was surrounded by his followers, and
that evening he was trying to tell them just how
much they were loved by God. It was as if Jesus
was sharing his Father's heart by saying that he
specially loved anyone who loved his Son. Today
we have access to that kind of a loving God.
Because we have expressed our love for his Son,
he is longing for ways to express his love for us
in return.

The secret to happiness and success is to accept them on God's terms.

This is the confidence we have in approaching God: that if we ask anything according to his will, he hears us. And if we know that he hears us—whatever we ask—we know that we have what we asked of him.   1 John 5:14-15

When we get our heart attuned to God's, we know we have what we ask. When we turn our life and will over to God, we have his promise that he will help us even to the point of working in us the desire to want all the right things and the ability to make good choices again. To be honest, we don't really know what is good for us, but God does, so we should ask him to adjust our values to what he says is good for us.

> **Sometimes the best way to help
> ourselves is to pray for others.**

*Admit your faults to one another and pray for
each other so that you may be healed. The ear-
nest prayer of a righteous man has great power
and wonderful results.*   James 5:16; TLB

After we have had a spiritual awakening, our
prayers and concern should be for those who
are also in need of deliverance. We need, however, to make certain that we are living in obedience to God so that our prayers will be effective.
Today, as we are concerned for our recovery
and healing, we can remember that God promises to help us as we are obedient and concerned
for others.

> **God gets glory from showing
> what he can do for us as a means
> of encouraging others to
> seek him also.**

*And I will do whatever you ask in my name, so
that the Son may bring glory to the Father. You
may ask me for anything in my name, and I will
do it.*   John 14:13-14

God loves to honor his Son, and the Son loves
to bring glory to his Father. Today, we need to
focus carefully on this truth, realizing that as we
allow Jesus Christ to control our life and to keep
us from sin, we are pleasing him and bringing
honor and glory to his Father.

Secret prayer brings open results.

When you pray, go into your room, close the door and pray to your Father, who is unseen. Then your Father, who sees what is done in secret, will reward you.   Matthew 6:6

Prayers that are prayed for others to hear go no higher than the ceiling. Dishonest testimonies about our deliverance only dishonor God, who wants us to be sincere at all times. If we really want to honor God, we will pray for his power in secret and show his power at work openly through our life.

Part Five

Dealing with Attitudes

*Here is a trustworthy saying
that deserves full acceptance:
Christ Jesus came into the
world to save sinners—of
whom I am the worst.*

1 Timothy 1:15

> **Being content today will do
> wonders for our body and spirit.**

A relaxed attitude lengthens a man's life; jealousy rots it away.　　　　Proverbs 14:30; TLB

Everything God has given us has to be considered as his estimate of our need at that moment. When envy bubbles to the surface, we are telling God that we aren't satisfied with his provision or don't trust his judgment. The best way to get through today is to accept what God has given and trust him to give us peace of heart and contentment with what he has supplied.

> **Understanding God's plan for
> our tomorrow helps us be
> content today.**

---

*Do not let your heart envy sinners, but always
be zealous for the fear of the Lord. There is
surely a future hope for you, and your hope will
not be cut off.*   Proverbs 23:17-18

Others seem to prosper for the moment, but
as we stay close to God and understand his will,
we will be able to see that the pleasures of sin
don't last, and that the only way to lasting peace
with God is to follow what we know to be his will
for us.

Today God wants us to be
content with something that is of
real value—godliness.

But godliness with contentment is great gain.
1 Timothy 6:6

One part of wisdom is gained only by experience: the ability to discern between the things
that bring lasting pleasure and those that offer
only temporary satisfaction—with a penalty to
be inflicted later. The more we study God's
Word and seek him through prayer and meditation, the more we will see that true joy and
peace will only come as we seek to please God.

The life of serenity Jesus
promises us day by day is more
than anyone else in the world
can give us.

*Then Jesus said to his disciples: "Therefore I tell
you, do not worry about your life, what you will
eat; or about your body, what you will wear. Life
is more than food, and the body more than
clothes."*
Luke 12:22-23

Food, clothing, and shelter—we learned many
years ago that these were the basic needs for life
on earth. God's Word tells us that even these are
not as important as our need to be certain that
our priorities are firmly fixed on doing God's
will. If we follow him, he takes care of everything else.

> **We need not worry about getting
> what we deserve—either now
> or in heaven.**

*Surely the righteous still are rewarded; surely
there is a God who judges the earth.*   Psalm 58:11

Trying to live for the kingdom of God while
still dealing with earthly matters day after day
sometimes makes it difficult to keep a proper
perspective. Sometimes we lose sight of heaven
and begin to envy those who are better off mate-
rially. Today we must remember whose we are,
where we are going, and who is really in control.

> **God's assurance that he
> will always be with us is more
> valuable than anything the
> world can offer us.**

*Keep your life free from the love of money and
be content with what you have, because God has
said, "Never will I leave you; never will I forsake you."*   Hebrews 13:5

God knows all about our needs, and he has
committed himself to providing for us. When we
see what money has done to change people we
know, we should perhaps be cautious about
envy, knowing that the things we desire might
cause us to take our eyes off God. Today we
need to recognize what it means to have God forever beside us and thank him for such a pre-
cious promise.

> When we are secure in God's
> presence, we have no desire to
> be a power-grabber.

Don't envy violent men. Don't copy their ways.
For such men are an abomination to the Lord,
but he gives his friendship to the godly.

Proverbs 3:31-32; TLB

People become violent when they fear that
something is being taken away from them. A violent person is usually trying to hang on to power.
God's perspective is one we ought to seek. God
promises today to make himself available to us
as we walk in his ways and seek to please him
with all we say and do.

5 / 7

> **Having God as our protector
> takes the worry out of day-to-day
> human relationships.**

*You will be protected from the lash of the tongue,
and need not fear when destruction comes.*

Job 5:21

When relationships with those around us
deteriorate, we begin to react in self-protective
ways. Knowing our reputation could be ruined
by someone's vicious tongue, we sometimes go on
the defensive, forgetting that God protects us as
we commit our protection to him. Today our
best hope is God himself, who has committed
himself to our protection.

❧

> God promises us a worry-free
> day as long as we keep our mind
> focused on him.

*You will keep in perfect peace him whose mind is
steadfast, because he trusts in you.*

Isaiah 26:3

A wise sea captain doesn't allow the waves to
make him take his eye off the compass or the
guiding star by which he is steering his ship.
God wants us to keep our heart fixed on him. As
long as we know his eye is on us, and as long as
we keep our eyes on him today, we are guaran-
teed his peace and security.

> **Living right today is the best way
> for us to stay serene and
> worry-free.**

*The fruit of righteousness will be peace; the
effect of righteousness will be quietness and
confidence forever.*   Isaiah 32:17

Very little in the world today can offer us real
peace of mind and heart. Real peace comes only
from Christ, the Prince of Peace. God's pre-
scription for finding peace is clear; today if we
want to enter into the peace God promised us,
we must find it through our relationship to him.

> **All the troubling noises around us today can be drowned out by God's music ringing in our heart.**

The Lord your God is with you, he is mighty to save. He will take great delight in you, he will quiet you with his love, he will rejoice over you with singing. Zephaniah 3:17

A common source of stress for us comes from the tempting pull of old habits. Sometimes we feel we are all alone in the battle. God's Word to us today is, "God is with you; he is mighty to save."

> **The secret to finding peace today
> is in the Word he has given us.**

*I have told you these things, so that in me you
may have peace. In this world you will have
trouble. But take heart! I have overcome the
world.*   John 16:33

The final score is all that counts in athletic
competition. In our race through life, struggling
with temptation and worrisome situations, we
often lose sight of the final goal. Christ's Word
for us today is, "In me you may have peace."

5 / 12

> **Stressful trials are easier to cope
> with now that we know the
> ultimate consequences
> will be beneficial.**

*We also rejoice in our sufferings, because we
know that suffering produces perseverance; perseverance, character; and character, hope. And
hope does not disappoint us, because God has
poured out his love into our hearts by the Holy
Spirit, whom he has given us.* Romans 5:3-5

Sometimes when God is trying to help us grow,
when he is trying to show us how he trusts us in
certain stressful situations, we grumble and take
such testing as an insult. God knows what we
can endure, and even through the difficulties he
has a plan to make us better if we allow him to
do his work.

> **Peace of mind today will depend
> upon the one we allow to
> control our mind.**

*The mind of sinful man is death, but the mind
controlled by the Spirit is life and peace.*

Romans 8:6

The stress we often feel results from a combination of pressures coming at us all at once. In the skirmish with these frustrations, we sometimes lose perspective and forget the Holy Spirit's willingness to restore the peace of God in our life. As we submit our life and will to God today, we need to let him have control of our mind, where this frustrating struggle is going on. God promises us peace today; we must accept it and thank him for it.

> One way to deal with stress is
> to fret over it ourselves;
> the other way—the way that
> works—is to turn the problem
> over to God and thank him.

*Do not be anxious about anything, but in every-
thing, by prayer and petition, with thanksgiving, present your requests to God.*

Philippians 4:6

There is a story of a man who was creeping on
hands and knees across a frozen river, fearing
the ice would break under his weight. He pan-
icked when he heard a terrible noise behind
him, thinking it was the ice in the river breaking
up. Turning around he saw a team of horses and
a heavily laden wagon rumbling confidently
across the frozen river. Sometimes our fears are
like that man's. God says he can care for us, and
he will.

> Anger means we are trying to
> take control; gentle answers
> mean we are trusting God.

*A gentle answer turns away wrath, but a harsh
word stirs up anger.* Proverbs 15:1

We are responsible not only for what we say,
but also for the emotional climate we create
around us by the way we say it. God wants us to
be like him—gentle and loving. He has made it
possible through his indwelling Spirit to produce
gentleness in us. He has promised today, and
every day, that he will go with us and help us to
be all that he wants us to be.

> **With God's peace controlling our
> heart today, we can change
> turmoil into tranquility.**

*A hot-tempered man stirs up dissension, but a
patient man calms a quarrel.*   Proverbs 15:18

Emotions are hard to analyze. Many times
we react in anger, not fully understanding why.
We need God's Spirit to work patience in our
life today. The world has enough quarrelsome
people. Let us ask God to help us calm the
quarrels.

> **Knowing God has forgiven us will make forgiving others today a simpler task.**

For if you forgive men when they sin against you, your heavenly Father will also forgive you.
Matthew 6:14

It may seem a difficult task, but the act of making amends where possible to people we have offended bears with it the promise of great benefit. Some of our loved ones who we thought were too offended to ever receive us again may be overwhelmed with tenderness toward us once we show them we really are sorry. The greatest promise, however, is the one God makes to us today.

> God promises to hear us, but our
> heart must let go of all the
> old hate.

---

*And when you stand praying, if you hold any-
thing against anyone, forgive him, so that your
Father in heaven may forgive you your sins.*

                                          Mark 11:25

Taking a moral inventory of our life creates
for some of us a long list of people whose forgiveness we need to seek. Our former sins and abu-
sive behavior often made us suspicious of
people, because of their reactions to our behavior. As a result, we became tense and quick-
tempered with them. Many old offenses need to
be forgiven on both sides. This verse, then,
should be a great encouragement for today.

> **We are forgiven! Realizing such
> love has been poured out on us
> will fill us with kindness and
> compassion toward others.**

*Be kind and compassionate to one another, for-
giving each other, just as in Christ God forgave
you.*   Ephesians 4:32

The more we learn about God through prayer
and meditation on his Word, the more we understand how compassionate he is. Time and time
again throughout history, his people rebelled
and fell into sin. And each time, when they
returned to him, he accepted and forgave them.
God's forgiving nature should make us very ten-
der toward those who have offended us. If God
can forgive like that, certainly he can help us to
be forgiving also.

Today we can prove how wise
God has made us by the way we
turn anger into peace.

*Mockers stir up a city, but wise men turn away
anger.*   Proverbs 29:8

We have all heard someone making excuses
for a bad temper by saying, "Sorry, I just lost
my head." Such a remark might be more true
than the person intends—the person didn't
actually lose his or her head, but the behavior
suggests that his or her head wasn't being used
wisely. God wants to make us wise, and today he
can help us to be wise in the way we control our
temper.

God's Spirit in us will give
us control today; there will be no
need for an angry outburst.

*A fool gives full vent to his anger, but a wise man
keeps himself under control.*   Proverbs 29:11

We hear another expression from those who
have exploded in anger: "I just lost my temper."
It is a very appropriate expression. Well-
tempered metal holds its shape, its firmness,
and its sharpness. A person who has lost his or
her temper has none of these qualities. God
wants us to be wise today; his Spirit in us desires
to keep us submissive to his control.

> **Fear is one of the major
> hindrances to faith; today we can
> cast off fear, knowing God is
> beside us, providing for us.**

*Even though I walk through the valley of the
shadow of death, I will fear no evil, for you are
with me; your rod and your staff, they comfort
me. You prepare a table before me in the presence of my enemies. You anoint my head with oil;
my cup overflows.*   Psalm 23:4-5

Lack of faith shows up in our fears. Whatever
causes us to fear defines us as far as our trust in
God is concerned. If we really believe the Good
Shepherd is with us, protecting us, meeting all
our needs, defeating our enemies, then we have
nothing to fear. If we continue to fear, it means
we don't really believe God's promise of such
care and protection.

Today's trouble won't strike
fear in our heart if we remember
that God is beside us in our
sorrow and adversity.

*God is our refuge and strength, an ever-present
help in trouble. Therefore we will not fear,
though the earth give way and the mountains
fall into the heart of the sea, though its waters
roar and foam and the mountains quake with
their surging.* Psalm 46:1-3

Natural calamities, such as earthquakes, hur-
ricanes, and tidal waves give us cause for nor-
mal fear. The psalmist pictures even these as not
worthy of our fear. God has promised to be our
refuge, our place of safety. When the storm
rages today, we must remember that our place
of safety is in God's presence.

> We won't fear the path through
> today because the one who
> always sees us is watching over us
> every step of the way.

*He will never let me stumble, slip, or fall. For he
is always watching, never sleeping. Jehovah himself is caring for you! He is your defender.*
Psalm 121:3-5; TLB

During combat, many soldiers stuck in fox-
holes were given a chance to sleep, while others
of their comrades were supposed to stay awake
and on guard. Fearful that these men on guard
might themselves fall asleep, many soldiers
stayed awake all night. Because we know the one
to whom we have committed our life and will is
faithful, we can rest comfortably today, knowing
who is in control and on guard.

> Safety today depends not on us
> and our strength and wisdom,
> but on the God in whom we have
> put our trust.

*Fear of man will prove to be a snare, but who-
ever trusts in the Lord is kept safe.*

Proverbs 29:25

When we fear people and things, we imply
they are more powerful than God, who told us
not to be afraid. Fear is a loss of perspective of
who and *whose* we are. God has promised to
keep safe all those who have committed themselves to his care. Let us prove our love and
trust in God today by putting fear aside.

> **God's word for today is**
> **"Fear not!" His word for us**
> **every day is "Fear not!"**

For I am the Lord, your God, who takes hold of
your right hand and says to you, Do not fear; I
will help you.   Isaiah 41:13

The right hand is the weapon hand; if God
holds our right hand, he doesn't intend for us to
do the fighting, but to leave it to him. Today we
have the promise that God is here with us to
hold our hand and to be our defense.

> No one in the world can send
> terror into our heart as long
> as we recognize and accept God's
> promise of protection
> and comfort.

I, even I, am he who comforts you. Who are you that you fear mortal men, the sons of men, who are but grass.   Isaiah 51:12

We know many dependable men and women, but none so dependable as God himself. Once we have committed ourselves to his care, we have the comfort of knowing he is able to meet all our needs. Today, as we face many obstacles, potential dangers, and perhaps even pain, we can thank God that he has promised to go through the day with us—as Comforter, Protector, and Friend.

Fear keeps us from stepping out
to conquer new territory; trust in
God today will take away all the
terror of the unknown.

*So we say with confidence, "The Lord is my
helper; I will not be afraid. What can man do to
me?"*   Hebrews 13:6

We put locks on our doors, our valuables in
strongboxes. But all of us know that no lock or
door can keep out someone who is fully intent on
taking from us or doing us harm. We have only
one safe place in the world, and that is in God's
presence. We need not be afraid today if we
have made God our place of refuge.

> **If Jesus said we are not to worry,
> then today he means for us
> to be unafraid.**

Peace I leave with you; my peace I give you. I do not give to you as the world gives. Do not let your hearts be troubled and do not be afraid.

John 14:27

Jesus told us not to let ourselves be troubled, as if it is a matter of our choice. More than we realize, we do decide whether our trust is going to rest in God's keeping power or in our own ability to keep ourselves safe. God wants to give us peace of mind and heart; as we seek to know him through his Word, we will understand that he is worthy of our trust.

Part Six

A New Start

So if you faithfully obey the commands I am giving you today—to love the Lord your God and to serve him with all your heart and with all your soul—then I will send rain on your land in its season, both autumn and spring rains, so that you may gather in your grain, new wine and oil.

Deuteronomy 11:13-14

> We can believe with certainty
> that God's work in us
> means a new start.

---

*See, I am doing a new thing! Now it springs up;
do you not perceive it? I am making a way in the
desert and streams in the wasteland.*   Isaiah 43:19

Remorse often keeps us from trying to
recover. A damaged record among all our
friends makes it an uphill battle to regain their
respect. But we have God's promise today that
as far as he is concerned, the past has been
put behind us; we have a brand-new start, and
this time with God as our helper.

> **The old person you were is gone;**
> **God says you are a new person.**

The nations will see your righteousness, and all kings your glory; you will be called by a new name that the mouth of the Lord will bestow.

Isaiah 62:2

When God finishes his work in us, many of our own friends may not recognize us. God isn't in the business of reconditioning old, tired, broken lives, as ours became as a result of all we have suffered. He is in the renewal business. Today he promises us new life, a new name, a new purpose, and new strength to be the person he wants us to be.

We are all subject to failure, but
God can give us a new start and
make us useful again.

Simon, Simon, Satan has asked to sift you as
wheat. But I have prayed for you, Simon, that
your faith may not fail. And when you have
turned back, strengthen your brothers.

Luke 22:31-32

All of our struggles prove just how helpless we
have become. Now that we have turned our life
over to God's control, we are still helpless, but
as Jesus prayed for Simon Peter, so he prays for
us that we won't fail. The Father hears the prayers of his Son—that is the promise we have for
today.

> **We tried before in our own effort; now God wants us to start again by the power of his Spirit.**

For what the law was powerless to do in that it was weakened by the sinful nature, God did by sending his own Son in the likeness of sinful man to be a sin offering. And so he condemned sin in sinful man, in order that the righteous requirements of the law might be fully met in us, who do not live according to the sinful nature but according to the Spirit.   Romans 8:3-4

The work of Christ on our behalf has cleared our record before God the Father and made it possible for us to begin again. The world may continue to hold things against us, even though we may have tried to make amends as much as possible, but today we can thank God that he sends us out with a clean slate.

We have a new record; Christ
has given us his perfect record to
make a new start possible.

God made him who had no sin to be sin for us,
so that in him we might become the righteous-
ness of God.   2 Corinthians 5:21

We didn't deserve it; we could never earn it;
yet God has chosen to forgive us based on his
grace and goodness. What Christ did for us on
the cross makes it possible for us to begin again,
knowing that our sins have been forgiven. Forgiven people, as we are, are prepared to face the
world again.

> **The difference between what we**
> **were before and what we are now**
> **is like the difference between**
> **death and life.**

When you were dead in your sins and in the
uncircumcision of your sinful nature, God made
you alive with Christ.   Colossians 2:13

Once we turned our life over to God's control
he brought about changes that we could never
earn or deserve. The difference now is that we
have the tremendous privilege of allowing the
life of Christ to live in us day by day. That is better than a new start—for us it is a new life.

> **A reborn person should be
> different, feel different,
> and act different.**

*But when the kindness and love of God our
Savior appeared, he saved us, not because of
righteous things we had done, but because of his
mercy. He saved us through the washing of
rebirth and renewal by the Holy Spirit, whom
he poured out on us generously through Jesus
Christ our Savior.*   Titus 3:4-6

For a long time we tried to reform, to put away
the destructive behavior that entrapped us. But
reformation wasn't the answer; what we needed
was a rebirth, a new life, which Christ gave to us
when we received him. Today we go forth not as
a reformed person, but as a reborn person, with
new power, new hope, and a new relationship
with our heavenly Father.

> **God will continue to change us to
> make us more like him.**

The God of all grace, who called you to his eternal glory in Christ, after you have suffered a little while, will himself restore you and make you strong, firm and steadfast.   1 Peter 5:10

The moment we received Christ into our life, we became a new creation. Because of the renewed spirit within us, we could wish that everything would change instantly, that all the old habits and sinful thoughts would disappear. God's work in that area of our life takes time. While we have the power to change, we don't always cooperate with God as we should. Today he promises to help us be strong and steadfast. We must take him at his word and thank him for his help.

> Our relationship to God has
> removed our cause for shame.

---

*Then I would not be put to shame when I con-
sider all your commands.*   Psalm 119:6

The behavior that brought us shame can now
be a thing of the past as we allow God's Word to
guide us. As we seek to know God through his
Word, the Holy Spirit uses its powerful message
to equip us for our struggles against temptation
and sin. Today we must thank God for his Word
and allow it to have its effect on our life.

> We have no fear of what people
> think of us as long as we are
> obeying God.

May my heart be blameless toward your decrees,
that I may not be put to shame.   Psalm 119:80

Old habits first took away our power to control our life; then they took away our self-respect. As we began to recover, the memories of our past life filled us with shame. But God, in removing the sin, wants also to remove the shame. Today we must allow his Word to have its effect so that we can proudly go on in victory, rejoicing in what God has done for us.

> **The Holy Spirit in us is our source of encouragement and our deliverance from shame.**

And hope does not disappoint us, because God has poured out his love into our hearts by the Holy Spirit, whom he has given us. **Romans 5:5**

God wants us to be happy, but he has linked happiness with holy living. The Holy Spirit enables us to love as God loves us. God's acceptance of us affirms just how valuable we are to him. Feeling shameful is not becoming to one who is loved by the Creator. Today let's put away remorse and joyfully accept God's forgiveness and love.

> Those who scoff at us will
> one day regret it; our trust is in
> God, who will help us hold
> our head up high.

*As it is written: "See, I lay in Zion a stone that
causes men to stumble and a rock that makes
them fall, and the one who trusts in him will
never be put to shame."*   Romans 9:33

Failure brings shame, especially when we
didn't have to fail. But we have placed the control of our life in the hands of a God who can
care for us, forgive us, and help us return to
sane living. As long as we are building on the
foundation with God as our cornerstone, we
never need to feel shame again.

> We used to be prisoners to sin,
> but now, as children of God, we
> have nothing to be ashamed of.

For you did not receive a spirit that makes you a slave again to fear, but you received the Spirit of sonship. And by him we cry, "Abba, Father."

Romans 8:15

The Spirit of God that dwells in us puts within us the sense that we are part of God's family. When we received him into our life we were born into his family. Before we feared him as an angry God; now we call him Father in the most intimate terms: "Abba."

> Knowing with certainty that our
> future is secure removes all
> concern about how we appear—
> to God or to others.

*I am not ashamed, because I know whom I have
believed, and am convinced that he is able to
guard what I have entrusted to him for that day.*
2 Timothy 1:12

Everyone loves to hear success stories. People
who have overcome great obstacles and personal
handicaps are admired by all of us. Today, as
we trust God to keep us away from the sins and
habits that had us in bondage, we can put away
our shame and become one of those success
stories.

> **Suffering isn't always our fault,**
> **but we should make sure that we**
> **aren't suffering for something**
> **we deserve.**

However, if you suffer as a Christian, do not be ashamed, but praise God that you bear that name.   1 Peter 4:16

As long as there are those who refuse God's rule over their lives, those who do want to please God are going to be mocked. It is a shame to be caught in wrongdoing and be rebuked publicly. But God says we should be proud if we suffer because we love God and are trying to live to please him.

> A renewed relationship to God
> means we can learn how
> to love again.

*Delight yourself in the Lord and he will give you
the desires of your heart.*   Psalm 37:4

As our relationship to God becomes secure,
our heart, once hardened by sin and rebellion,
becomes soft and sensitive again. Emotions long
deadened by old sinful habits are awakened.
Enjoying God's love stimulates us to love others.
The love God gives us is both a command and a
promise for us today.

Nothing generates more feelings
of love than being loved—and
God loves you!

*As a young man marries a maiden, so will your
sons marry you; as a bridegroom rejoices over
his bride, so will your God rejoice over you.*

Isaiah 62:5

When we continue to disobey our conscience,
the less sensitive that delicate gift from God
becomes. When the conscience becomes seared,
very often all other emotions become deadened
as well. But God's love awakens not only our
conscience, but our ability to love others. Just
think what it means to us today to know that
God delights in us!

We will never understand how to
love until we fathom the depths
of God's love for us.

*I will heal their waywardness and love them
freely, for my anger has turned away from
them.*   Hosea 14:4

Unloved people find it hard to love others.
But that is not the case with us—we are dearly
loved by a forgiving, loving God. What better
way for us to respond than to share the overflow
of his love with others today!

> **The Father wants his love for his Son to be our example as we love one another.**

I [Jesus] have made you known to them, and will continue to make you known in order that the love you have for me may be in them and that I myself may be in them.

John 17:26

When Jesus spoke this prayer, he was standing between two worlds: the world where his beloved disciples lived, and the world of his heavenly Father, to whom he was soon to return. In that position, Jesus was forging a link between the two worlds; the love he shared with his Father he was going to extend to us, so that we can love as he loves. Today we have the privilege of sharing that love with others.

> **We are alive again; able to love
> again because of God's renewing
> work in our heart.**

*But because of his great love for us, God, who is
rich in mercy, made us alive with Christ even
when we were dead in transgressions—it is by
grace you have been saved. And God raised us
up with Christ and seated us with him in the
heavenly realms in Christ Jesus, in order that in
the coming ages he might show the incomparable
riches of his grace, expressed in his kindness to
us in Christ Jesus.*   Ephesians 2:4-7

Christ's life in us makes us alive to love the
people around us today, as Christ loves them
and gave his life for them.

> **God promises that his Spirit in us**
> **will be the power source of our**
> **love for one another.**

For God did not give us a spirit of timidity, but a spirit of power, of love and of self-discipline.
                                                        2 Timothy 1:7

We thought we knew how to love before God took control of our life. Most of us must now admit that our love was usually in response to someone else's love, or to get love in return. Only the Holy Spirit in us enables us to love unconditionally. Today we have an opportunity to allow God's Spirit to express his love through us to those around us.

> God promises to make his love
> flow through us to others.

*If anyone acknowledges that Jesus is the Son of
God, God lives in him and he in God. And so we
know and rely on the love God has for us. God is
love. Whoever lives in love lives in God, and God
in him.*   1 John 4:15-16

We prove—not only to the world, but to
ourselves—our relationship to God by the way
we love. If we love as God does, then we know
that God lives in us. If we are trusting in him
today, then we reflect it by showing love to him
in obedience and showing love to others in
service and respect.

> **It was God's love that redeemed
> us, giving us new life and a new
> heart of love for others.**

We love because he first loved us.　　　John 4:19

We don't love God to pay him back for loving us—that is not the meaning of this verse. We love God because he loved us enough to give us new life and a new spirit, and with it the ability to love him. His love in us makes us able to be a channel of his love to others.

> **Realizing what we are in God's
> sight does wonders for our
> battered self-esteem.**

*You made him a little lower than the heavenly
beings and crowned him with glory and honor.*
                                                Psalm 8:5

Many of us grew up listening to very damag-
ing messages from our parents and peers, saying
how worthless we were. The old messages keep
playing in our mind like a tape recording. These
old messages are best erased by seeking God
through meditation on his Word. As we do, we
discover his perspective; we understand what
value God places on us. That is a message we
need to tell ourselves today as we seek to erase
all the old lies we heard about ourselves.

> **Who of us can feel bad about
> ourselves when God calls
> us his friends!**

*I no longer call you servants, because a servant
does not know his master's business. Instead, I
have called you friends, for everything that I
learned from my Father I have made known to
you.*   John 15:15

A hard-working servant has nothing to be
ashamed of; God honors us for honest work.
But how much more honorable it is to be considered not a servant, but a son or daughter of
God—and even beyond that, a friend of his!

Now that we are God's children, he is making us look more and more like him!

And we, who with unveiled faces all reflect the Lord's glory, are being transformed into his likeness with ever-increasing glory, which comes from the Lord, who is the Spirit. 2 Corinthians 3:18

Some people claim that as a loving couple grows older, they sometimes begin to look like one another. Someone said, "We grow into the image of the ones we love." That is what God allows for us. The more we know him and love him, the more we want to look and act like him as much as we can.

> **Knowing we are God's children
> makes us want to live up
> to the name.**

*You are all sons of God through faith in Christ
Jesus.*   Galatians 3:26

A story, perhaps apocryphal, was told, that
Alexander the Great scolded a cowardly soldier
also named Alexander by saying, "Change your
behavior or change your name!" Being called a
child of God gives us great encouragement to be
like our heavenly Father. Being a child of God
also endows us with the power to grow more and
more into his image.

> **Remembering that we
> are children of God will make a
> difference in how we feel
> about ourselves.**

*So you are no longer a slave, but a son; and
since you are a son, God has made you also an
heir.*   Galatians 4:7

It matters little what others think of us as long
as we know what God has said about us. Our
self-esteem is not based on what we can do in
our own effort; our abilities got us into nothing
but trouble and bondage. Our self-respect
comes from what God has done for us and what
he now says is true of us.

> **Being a child of God means
> we always know where home is
> and that we have brothers
> and sisters everywhere.**

*Consequently, you are no longer foreigners and
aliens, but fellow citizens with God's people and
members of God's household.* Ephesians 2:19

Once we became a child of God a number of
changes took place. We received a new Father
and a new family. We received new citizenship
papers—we are now citizens of heaven. We
received a new home, and someday we will be
there, enjoying the presence of our Father and
the love and friendship of all our brothers and
sisters in Christ. These thoughts should make a
difference in how we think about ourselves
today.

> **Like a master architect,
> our Creator has visualized a
> beautiful plan of what he
> wants us to become.**

*In him the whole building is joined together and
rises to become a holy temple in the Lord. And in
him you too are being built together to become a
dwelling in which God lives by his Spirit.*

Ephesians 2:21-22

Recovering from the pain brought on by
uncontrollable elements in our past, we tend
to get impatient, hoping for better and faster
progress. Today we need to remember that the
Creator, who is also our Redeemer, is in the
midst of a building project, which is our life.
We need to be grateful that he knows what we
need, and in his time he will complete his work
in us.

Part Seven

===

Making Good Choices

*Even strong young lions some-
times go hungry, but those of
us who reverence the Lord
will never lack any good
thing.* Psalm 34:10; TLB

God works in us to bring us
to maturity.

*Now I commit you to God and to the word of his
grace, which can build you up and give you an
inheritance among all those who are sanctified.*
Acts 20:32

Children at first don't understand everything their parents compel them to do. A well-
nurtured child returns in adulthood to thank his
parents for their insistence on good discipline,
which produced growth. In adulthood, the good
habits of childhood continue. It is this kind of
work the Holy Spirit wants to do in us day by
day, to bring us to a mature, successful, prosperous life. God promises to help us today to that
end if we let him.

> We know we are coming to full recovery when we are finding the inner strength to stand alone, depending on nothing but our relationship to God.

Make it your ambition to lead a quiet life, to mind your own business and to work with your hands, just as we told you, so that your daily life may win the respect of outsiders and so that you will not be dependent on anybody.

1 Thessalonians 4:11-12

It was right for us to depend on others during our recovery; now, as we mature, we should be reaching out to others. That is the goal toward which we are working, and God wants to help us today.

> **Our confidence in God grows as
> we put our trust in him and
> find him faithful.**

*Dear friends, if our hearts do not condemn us,
we have confidence before God and receive from
him anything we ask, because we obey his commands and do what pleases him.*   1 John 3:21-22

Growing up spiritually means becoming more
internally motivated toward good choices. Walking in obedience to all the light God gives us
today not only brings peace of mind and heart,
but also gives us a profitable day and makes us
an example of what God can do, an encouragement to others to trust in him.

> **Understanding God's will for our
> life gives direction and purpose.**

*The Lord will fulfill his purpose for me; your
love, O Lord, endures forever—do not abandon
the works of your hands.*   Psalm 138:8

Unless we develop some mature goals, we wan-
der aimlessly through life, are caught off guard
by temptation, and easily fall back into the old,
addictive life patterns. Knowing to whom we
belong and knowing what kind of life God
desires for us keeps us on a steady, solid growth
pattern. Let us make today another step toward
progress and maturity.

> **Growing toward maturity is a process; no one achieves it overnight or without patience and endurance.**

For this very reason, make every effort to add to your faith goodness; and to goodness, knowledge; and to knowledge, self-control; and to self-control, perseverance; and to perseverance, godliness; and to godliness, brotherly kindness; and to brotherly kindness, love. For if you possess these qualities in increasing measure, they will keep you from being ineffective and unproductive in your knowledge of our Lord Jesus Christ.   2 Peter 1:5-8

God says to us today, "Make every effort." He will take care of the rest of our growth and development.

> The mature qualities of life—
> love, discernment, and wisdom—
> will develop as we allow the
> Holy Spirit to control us.

*And this is my prayer: that your love may
abound more and more in knowledge and depth
of insight, so that you may be able to discern
what is best and may be pure and blameless until
the day of Christ, filled with the fruit of righteousness that comes through Jesus Christ—to
the glory and praise of God.*   Philippians 1:9-11

As a child, we were compelled to do many
things we didn't like at the time. Now we can see
that God's plan is for our obedience to him to
produce a happier, more exciting, and profitable life. At the same time, we bring honor and
praise to God.

> **The Word of God, as it is given
> a place in our life, has
> power in itself to produce
> growth and maturity.**

All over the world this gospel is bearing fruit and growing, just as it has been doing among you since the day you heard it and understood God's grace in all its truth.
Colossians 1:6

Prayer and meditation on his Word are as important to our spiritual growth as good soil, water, and sunlight are to the growth of a plant. Spiritual maturity comes as we do what we need to do without external coercion. Today God wants us to allow his Word to have a nurturing effect on us. He promises to bless our efforts.

There is a close connection
between knowing, obeying,
and growing.

*Whatever you have learned or received or heard
from me, or seen in me—put it into practice.
And the God of peace will be with you.*

Philippians 4:9

It does little good to make promises and com-
mitments without the determination to follow
up on them. God goes with us along the path
of progress; his promise of protection and support does not necessarily follow us when we
lapse into our old way of life. We have today his
promise of peace; all we need to do is accept it.

**Continuing to do what we know
is right is the surest way
to grow stronger.**

---

*The righteous will hold to their ways, and those
with clean hands will grow stronger.* Job 17:9

In the Christian life, we either move forward
or begin to slip. Clean hands mean a clean
heart; when we know of people we have harmed,
we need to apologize, and keep our record
straight with God and man. God blesses us and
helps us grow stronger as we exercise ourselves
toward spiritual growth.

> **Success in recovery depends
> on our commitment to pleasing
> the one in whom we have
> put our trust.**

*Fear the Lord, you his saints, for those who fear
him lack nothing. The lions may grow weak and
hungry, but those who seek the Lord lack no
good thing.*   Psalm 34:9-10

When we commit our life and will to God, we
relinquish the responsibility we have felt to control ourselves. As we maintain our perspective
on where we are, we will remember that it was
our loss of control that pointed out our need for
God to enter our life. Now that he has control,
we no longer need to fear, for we are promised—
today and every day—his provision of all our
needs.

> **Each day the light on the path
> grows brighter, the longer
> we are committed to staying on
> course with God.**

*The path of the righteous is like the first gleam
of dawn, shining ever brighter till the full light of
day.*   Proverbs 4:18

As we follow the light God gives us today, we
will find ourselves flooded with more and more
light. Following the light is more than following a
direction; it is accepting the light as truth and
making the commitment to live it out moment by
moment. God's light today will be bright enough
to see each step we need to take today.

God chose us and planted good
seed in our heart, and the
Holy Spirit continues his
cultivation in order that we might
be fruit bearers.

My true disciples produce bountiful harvests.
This brings great glory to my Father.

John 15:8; TLB

Once crops begin to grow, the process does
not reverse itself. So it is with our spiritual life;
we prove the quality of the plant by the fruit it
produces. In the same way we show ourselves to
be of God by the fruit our life produces. God
promises to work through us today to produce
good fruit.

The more we look at Jesus, love him, and try to be like him, the more we will look like him.

And we, who with unveiled faces all reflect the Lord's glory, are being transformed into his likeness with ever-increasing glory, which comes from the Lord, who is the Spirit.

2 Corinthians 3:18

By staying close to God and his Word through prayer and meditation, we take on godly qualities. God's goal is to one day transform our body and soul into the image of his Son. Day by day, as we seek to know God better we have the promise that changes—perhaps not at first observable—healthy adjustments are taking place within our heart and life.

> **Until we are in heaven, the
> growth process must continue.**

*Finally, brothers, we instructed you how to live
in order to please God, as in fact you are living.
Now we ask you and urge you in the Lord Jesus
to do this more and more.* 1 Thessalonians 4:1

Some people seem to stop growing, mentally
and spiritually, about the time they quit growing
physically. What a tragedy! Others seem to be
on the growth curve almost till the day they die.
Each day God wants us to claim his grace and
grow to be more like him.

> **God promises to give us all we
> need to be all we should be.**

*It was he who gave some to be apostles, some to
be prophets, some to be evangelists, and some to
be pastors and teachers . . . so that the body of
Christ may be built up . . . and become mature,
attaining to the whole measure of the fullness of
Christ.*   Ephesians 4:11-13

We should never compare ourselves with
others and the talents God has given them. He
has a job for us, and we are wise to compare ourselves only in terms of what God has given us to
do and how well we do it. We have the promise
from God that he has supplied us with all we
need to do what he wants done today.

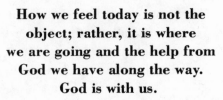

How we feel today is not the
object; rather, it is where
we are going and the help from
God we have along the way.
God is with us.

He who stands firm to the end will be saved.

Matthew 24:13

As we examine our life, we may grow impatient with how far we have to go to be the person we want to be. We must remember that God is measuring our progress, our desire to grow, and how far we have come. His word for us today is, "Stand firm; keep moving onward."

> **Moving toward the goal of full recovery is also progress toward our eternal rest, which is to be found in God's presence.**

That is why I am suffering as I am. Yet I am not ashamed, because I know whom I have believed, and am convinced that he is able to guard what I have entrusted to him for that day.

2 Timothy 1:12

The pain of progress will be repaid by the pleasure of accomplishment. God desires that we keep growing and stay patient in the process.

> **Progress is sometimes slow,**
> **so we must be patient today,**
> **keeping the goal in focus.**

Then, knowing what lies ahead for you, you won't become bored with being a Christian nor become spiritually dull and indifferent, but you will be anxious to follow the example of those who receive all that God has promised them because of their strong faith and patience.

Hebrews 6:12; TLB

In early spring, the crocus peeps up quickly from the ground, blossoms beautifully for a few days or weeks, and is gone. The oak tree takes years to come from the acorn, several years longer as a struggling shrub, and sometimes centuries before it stands tall to spread its shade over the land. While we are prone to want instant success, God wants to give us oak-tree patience.

We are not alone in our struggle
for recovery. God is with us
and strengthens us for
each day's journey.

*Let us hold unswervingly to the hope we profess,
for he who promised is faithful.*   Hebrews 10:23

One of the highest compliments we can give
a person is to say, "He's as good as his word."
In a world of broken promises and unkept
pledges, it is a comfort to know that God, the
perfectly faithful one, has promised to go with
us all the way.

> **God has begun a work in us.**
> **Like good seed in fertile soil, it**
> **will come to full fruit in time.**

Be patient, then, brothers, until the Lord's com-
ing. See how the farmer waits for the land to
yield its valuable crop and how patient he is for
the autumn and spring rains. You too, be patient
and stand firm, because the Lord's coming is
near.   James 5:7-8

Bad habits develop slowly, almost impercepti-
bly. Good habits may take quite awhile also, but
as a farmer waits for grain to grow, we should be
patient and trust God for a plentiful harvest of
blessing.

> **Great profit can come from hard
> times; if we choose to respond
> to it properly, testing can
> make us better people.**

*Consider it pure joy, my brothers, whenever you
face trials of many kinds, because you know
that the testing of your faith develops perseverance. Perseverance must finish its work so that
you may be mature and complete, not lacking
anything.* James 1:2-4

The laurels of victory are the capstone of
many months—sometimes years—of hard discipline and perseverance. The victor's crown
makes it all seem worthwhile. And so it will be
for us when we reach full recovery.

God honors us for having the
right attitude when we
suffer wrongly.

*But how is it to your credit if you receive a beat-
ing for doing wrong and endure it? But if you
suffer for doing good and you endure it, this is
commendable before God.*   1 Peter 2:20

Earth is not heaven; people are not perfect;
we will suffer many wrongs we don't deserve.
God considers our reactions to all these. He is
committed to our protection, and he is the
rewarder and judge of good and evil. Today, as
we turn our life over to his control, we can feel
secure in his love.

> We have a bright future before
> us now that we have given God
> control of our life.

*If they obey and serve him, they will spend the
rest of their days in prosperity and their years in
contentment.*   Job 36:11

The pursuit of God and his holiness would be
depressing if we didn't know that God was
aware of our inability to achieve his standards.
His work of grace through Jesus was to make it
possible for him to give us a new heart to seek
him and a new spirit to empower us. Success
and recovery come as we allow him to do his
work in us, and as we cooperate with his Spirit
in obeying all we know of his will today.

**Most things that are good for us
are worth waiting for.**

*Do not store up for yourselves treasures on
earth, where moth and rust destroy, and where
thieves break in and steal. But store up for yourselves treasures in heaven, where moth and rust
do not destroy, and where thieves do not break
in and steal.*   Matthew 6:19-20

We strive to gain wealth in this world, not realizing that all the things of such great value here
on earth are no more than paving material for
the streets of heaven. Only those things to which
God attaches value are of any worth to us and
deserving of our pursuits. Today, let us make a
new start in seeking those things that won't fade
away.

> We must say no to many things today if we want God's best for both today and tomorrow.

If anyone would come after me, he must deny himself and take up his cross and follow me. For whoever wants to save his life will lose it, but whoever loses his life for me will find it. What good will it be for a man if he gains the whole world, yet forfeits his soul? Or what can a man give in exchange for his soul?   Matthew 16:24-26

Saying no to all the old temptations that made us lose control of our life is the specific thing we must do today and every day as we seek to follow Christ. Of course, it is painful to say no to those things that our body and mind crave, but the prize is well worth the cost. Today, we must say no again and again to ourselves and follow Christ.

> The axiom "No pain, no gain"
> applies to our spiritual
> growth as well.

*Therefore, brothers, we have an obligation—but
it is not to the sinful nature, to live according to
it. For if you live according to the sinful nature,
you will die; but if by the Spirit you put to death
the misdeeds of the body, you will live.*

Romans 8:12-13

Any athlete must be willing to work against
the pain as he or she builds the muscles and
skills needed for perfection. Our encouragement
should come from the fact that the goal is
assured for us. There are no failures among
God's athletes who keep before them the goal of
pleasing their Creator and Lord.

> Many sweaty days are spent in
> the field before good grain
> is harvested.

Let us not become weary in doing good, for at
the proper time we will reap a harvest if we do
not give up.   Galatians 6:9

God is in the business of growing things—
grain, fruit from all kinds of trees, and spiritual
fruit in the lives of his children. It is the vision
of the harvest that keeps us steadfast. God
wants us to remember that he is as concerned as
we are that we grow to maturity, so he encourages us day by day to do our best and be patient.

7 / 27

> **Doing God's will takes a
> day-by-day commitment,
> requiring patience only a vision
> of God can give us.**

---

*You need to persevere so that when you have
done the will of God, you will receive what he
has promised.*   Hebrews 10:36

Some call it plodding; some call it enduring;
others call it a victorious walk with God every
day. Walking with God is never dull or boring.
Challenges come, but keeping the course day by
day leads to blessing, God's joyous fellowship,
and peace of mind.

> **Christ suffered to bring us joy;**
> **to enter into his joy we are**
> **sometimes called on to suffer**
> **with him—but with what**
> **great reward!**

Dear friends, do not be surprised at the painful
trial you are suffering, as though something
strange were happening to you. But rejoice that
you participate in the sufferings of Christ, so
that you may be overjoyed when his glory is
revealed.   1 Peter 4:12-13

By now we must realize that following Christ
isn't a walk through a rose garden. The joy of
the journey comes in knowing Christ suffered to
a degree that we never will, and that he is with
us to comfort, protect, and strengthen. And
what joy awaits us when the journey is over!

> **Making the decision to turn our
> life over to God's control means
> God's promises are ours—
> today and tomorrow.**

*"I tell you the truth," Jesus said to them, "no
one who has left home or wife or brothers or
parents or children for the sake of the kingdom
of God will fail to receive many times as much in
this age and, in the age to come, eternal life."*
Luke 18:29-30

The promise Jesus made to his disciples is
valid for each of us. We may feel that turning
our life over to God for his control was costly.
Only when the final goal is reached will we
understand what joys and benefits God has in
store for those who have chosen to follow him.

Part Eight

Finding Sources of Strength

And He has said to me, "My grace is sufficient for you, for power is perfected in weakness." Most gladly, therefore, I will rather boast about my weaknesses, that the power of Christ may dwell in me.

2 Corinthians 12:9; NASB

> **Following Christ is not a matter
> of knowing the way; it is a matter
> of being willing to be led.**

*In your unfailing love you will lead the people
you have redeemed. In your strength you will
guide them to your holy dwelling.*   Exodus 15:13

We often suggest that the process of finding
God's will is much harder than it really is. God
the Father loves us and wants us to follow him
in safe paths. Our difficulty is not in knowing
the way; it is in being willing to be teachable.
Today, God wants us to reach out for his hand
and follow.

> We should not be afraid
> to commit our will to our
> eternal Creator.

For this God is our God for ever and ever; he will be our guide even to the end.   Psalm 48:14

When our life went out of control, many of our friends weren't able to help us, so they left us to struggle alone. Feeling abandoned, we lost faith in people and wondered how permanent any relationship could be. God wants us to see that he is faithful; once we committed our life to him, he has become not only our Savior but our forever friend.

> Once we have decided to follow
> God's leading, he assumes
> responsibility to make the way
> clear to us.

Although the Lord gives you the bread of adversity and the water of affliction, your teachers will be hidden no more; with your own eyes you will see them. Whether you turn to the right or to the left, your ears will hear a voice behind you, saying, "This is the way; walk in it."

Isaiah 30:20-21

Guidance isn't a protracted timetable and road map, marking out the years and the miles ahead. Instead, God wants from us an attitude of dependence, a willingness to wait for his voice to give us guidance moment by moment.

> There is no such thing as
> unfamiliar territory with God
> as our guide.

*I will lead the blind by ways they have not
known, along unfamiliar paths I will guide
them; I will turn the darkness into light before
them and make the rough places smooth. These
are the things I will do; I will not forsake them.*

Isaiah 42:16

Making radical changes in our life causes
everything to seem strange. Our new life-style
makes us feel and act like a different person, in
a strange new world that has no familiar land-
marks. We must believe today that the one to
whom we committed our life is leading us day
by day.

> As long as we are willing to be
> led, God will teach us the way
> and guide us in it.

*I will instruct you and teach you in the way you
should go; I will counsel you and watch over
you.*   Psalm 32:8

Once we lost control of our life, good decisions
became more and more difficult to make. Learning to make good decisions again is part of the
recovery process. The best decision we can
make today is to turn our life over to God's control and let him lead us.

> God says, "Depend on me." He
> loves us and will take care of us.

*Yet I am always with you; you hold me by my
right hand. You guide me with your counsel, and
afterward you will take me into glory.*

Psalm 73:23-24

A child's attitude of dependence on a loving
father is a tribute to the sense of trust the parent has engendered in his child. Today, remember that a loving Father, with a spotless
reputation for being a loving and protecting
parent, is reaching out for your right hand.
He wants to lead you in the best possible path
for you.

> ## Those who belong to God don't lack wisdom and direction.

His God instructs him and teaches him the right way.   Isaiah 28:26

Finding God's direction means searching for it from the right sources. Daily prayer and meditation on God's Word are the means we are given—not only to know his will, but to find the loving encouragement we need to walk in the truth he shows us.

There is no need for us to be
ignorant when we have a
gracious God who wants to teach
us all we need to know.

*If any of you lacks wisdom, he should ask God,
who gives generously to all without finding fault,
and it will be given to him.*   James 1:5

Submission to God opens up a bright light
source for us. Wisdom from God is not a matter
of intelligence but of the will. Today, God wants
us to seek his wisdom. A loving Father delights
in children who are walking in the truth.

> **Compared with God's riches
> we were poor, but now he
> declares us rich, supplied from
> all he owns.**

From your bounty, O God, you provided for the poor.   Psalm 68:10

Turning our life around sometimes means starting anew in many areas of our life. Sometimes new associations cut us off from support we formerly enjoyed. When we choose to go God's way and turn our life over to him, he takes responsibility for protecting and providing for us.

> **God will keep his promise to provide for us who have put our trust in him.**

He provides food for those who fear him; he remembers his covenant forever.   Psalm 111:5

All human resources will, in the end, be depleted. We need a source of supply that is never exhausted, and that is what God wants to be for us. Once we commit our life to him, he, as a loving Father, promises to care for us forever.

> He is a faithful God; he is
> worthy of our trust. His
> reputation is intact.

*I was young and now I am old, yet I have never
seen the righteous forsaken or their children
begging bread.*   Psalm 37:25

We can't always depend on the loyalty of even
our most faithful friends. Yet, as we examine the
Scriptures and the testimony of those we know
who have followed Christ for many years, a
record of faithfulness emerges that should make
us unafraid to trust him today.

> Once we have come to know God
> through his Word, we learn
> how wise our choice was to turn
> our life and will over to him.

My soul will be satisfied as with the richest of foods; with singing lips my mouth will praise you.
Psalm 63:5

The picture of rich food spread before us, and a place of joyful singing, describes what it is like to enjoy pleasant fellowship with God our Father. We miss all of this if we aren't praying daily and getting to know our heavenly Father through meditating on his Word.

> We may experience dryness
> of soul now, but God has
> promised us a rich harvest with
> joy and fulfillment as we continue
> walking with him.

*They will come and shout for joy on the heights
of Zion; they will rejoice in the bounty of the
Lord—the grain, the new wine and the oil, the
young of the flocks and herds. They will be like a
well-watered garden, and they will sorrow no
more.*
Jeremiah 31:12

The human spirit can endure almost anything
as long as there is some end in sight. Before we
turned our life over to God for his care, we had
nothing but a dark prison cell of destructive
habits. We still suffer the effects of these problems, but God encourages us day by day with
hope for a bright tomorrow.

> **Some benefits are of greater
> worth than clothing and food.
> God's provision for us
> prepares us for an eternal
> wedding banquet.**

*I delight greatly in the Lord; my soul rejoices in
my God. For he has clothed me with garments of
salvation and arrayed me in a robe of righteousness, as a bridegroom adorns his head like a
priest, and as a bride adorns herself with her
jewels.*   Isaiah 61:10

Destructive living patterns took their toll on
our life, leaving us feeling worn and tattered.
But when God came into our life, he brought a
renewed spirit and heart. Today we can rejoice
in the splendid garments of righteousness he has
placed on us to prepare us for the upcoming
feast.

> **He promised us all we need for today; though some days are tear-filled, a joyful harvest awaits us.**

Those who sow in tears will reap with songs of joy. He who goes out weeping, carrying seed to sow, will return with songs of joy, carrying sheaves with him.   Psalm 126:5-6

Some have suggested that we would never really understand peace until we had suffered turmoil. The burdens of this life prepare us for the joyful future we are promised in God's kingdom.

> **Material blessings are a gift; but
> the greater gift is eternal wealth,
> which we have as a more
> precious gift from God.**

*Moreover, when God gives any man wealth and
possessions, and enables him to enjoy them, to
accept his lot and be happy in his work—this is
a gift of God.*   Ecclesiastes 5:19

Material wealth is not an end in itself. God
does, however, give us many things here on
earth to richly enjoy. Some of the material blessings we lost as a result of bad living habits of the
past. When God restores us, he often returns
some of these earthly blessings to encourage us
to seek wealth and pleasure beyond earthly
abundance—wealth that endures forever in
heaven.

> The more we get to know God,
> the more joy we have in seeing
> him as all we need.

*Surely then you will find delight in the Almighty
and will lift up your face to God.*   Job 22:26

When God turns our weakness into strength,
we have a new perspective on life. As we discover that through his power we can regain
control of our life, there is cause for joy. The
struggle goes on and sometimes seems endless,
but God's promise will lighten our spirit today.

> There is a big difference between
> the fleeting happiness this
> world offers and the real, eternal
> joy we discover through our
> relationship with God.

You have made known to me the path of life; you will fill me with joy in your presence, with eternal pleasures at your right hand. Psalm 16:11

When we seek God's will by spending time with him in prayer and the study of his Word, the light on the path grows stronger each day. His presence with us in our day-to-day struggle is cause for joy. Count on his guidance and presence today.

> As we grow closer to God,
> we learn that to suffer
> temporarily and to maintain a
> deep abiding joy in our
> relationship with him are not
> contradictory.

For his anger lasts only a moment, but his favor lasts a lifetime; weeping may remain for a night, but rejoicing comes in the morning.   Psalm 30:5

When we were children, those moments when our parents had to inflict punishment seemed to last for hours. Now we know that loving parents were as anxious to get the discipline finished as we were. God's discipline is no different. At the end, when the lesson is learned, God usually gives us some special token to show he is still our loving Father.

> **Having a right relationship
> with God gives us a reason
> to feel joyful.**

*Blessed are those who have learned to acclaim
you, who walk in the light of your presence, O
Lord. They rejoice in your name all day long;
they exult in your righteousness.*   Psalm 89:15-16

Walking in the light of God's wisdom, while
usually a pleasant experience, sometimes calls us
to take unpleasant turns. If we want to continue
enjoying the smile of God's presence, he may
ask us to amend some outstanding sin in our life.
We may have offended someone, and we need to
make amends in order to see God's smile again.
When he shows us what is right today, we must
do it.

> **When we walked in darkness,
> we had no reason for joy;
> God's light shining in our life has
> made the difference!**

*Light is shed upon the righteous and joy on the
upright in heart. Rejoice in the Lord, you who
are righteous, and praise his holy name.*

Psalm 97:11-12

Most people who are really trying to walk
with God in humility and righteousness are
usually more concerned about their pride and
sinfulness than others. They are the ones who
have put God's searchlight on their lives to see
if there are wrongs that need to be righted, sins
to be confessed, restitution to be made. Today,
don't be afraid of God's light.

> Knowing our sins have been
> paid for by Christ should gladden
> our heart each time we think
> about it.

*The ransomed of the Lord will return. They will
enter Zion with singing; everlasting joy will
crown their heads. Gladness and joy will overtake them, and sorrow and sighing will flee
away.*   Isaiah 51:11

Once we have found God and entered into all
the benefits of being his child, we can enjoy life
again, knowing the old way of life won't return
to hurt us or our loved ones again as long as we
continue following God. Our recovered life has a
way of showing others where they might find the
kind of joy and peace we have found. Today, we
should let our joy reach out to someone who
needs it.

> **Like the disciples, we wait for
> our Master's return. Sometimes
> the long wait, dealing with
> daily problems, isn't easy. But he
> is coming back again!**

*Now is your time of grief, but I will see you
again and you will rejoice, and no one will take
away your joy.*   John 16:22

The long struggle to be free from the effects of
past sins seems endless. Many people and situations discourage us, and our own impatience—
often the by-product of our former life-style—
makes the dark night seem even longer. But as
long as we know God is with us, we can find
courage and strength for one more day.

> ### Once we turn our life over to God, he becomes our safe place.

The Lord is my rock, my fortress and my deliverer; my God is my rock, in whom I take refuge. He is my shield and the horn of my salvation, my stronghold.   Psalm 18:2

Our decision to turn our life over to God guarantees us all the security we will ever need. No temptation can entrap us again as long as we are committed to doing God's will and accepting his plan for our life. Today we can count on his loving presence, his protection, and his power to say no to any temptation that may come our way.

> **Believing God's promise
> of protection will make this a
> brighter day.**

*Cast your cares on the Lord and he will sustain
you; he will never let the righteous fall.*

Psalm 55:22

Our past failures have caused us to lose confidence in ourselves. When we lost control of our life, we realized we needed God's help if we were ever to recover. A part of what God wants to do for us today is to give us the assurance of his love and protection. Knowing God is now on our side to help us rebuild our life gives us reason to believe in ourselves again.

Our Good Shepherd waits for us
to ask for his protection today.

The Lord is good, a refuge in times of trouble.
He cares for those who trust in him.   Nahum 1:7

When we invited God into our life, his searchlight of truth pointed out many of our shortcomings. The result for some of us was a total sense
of failure and defeat. God wants us to rise above
those feelings, accept his love and forgiveness,
and walk today under his protective shelter
from the things that could defeat us again.

> **God knows who we are and how
> we feel, and his arms are open
> today to give us what we need.**

*Come to me, all you who are weary and bur-
dened, and I will give you rest. Take my yoke
upon you and learn from me, for I am gentle
and humble in heart, and you will find rest for
your souls.*   Matthew 11:28-29

Many times we struggled to rise above the
past and the habits that nearly destroyed us.
Now we have God on our side, strengthening us
against the temptations that defeated us in the
past. Today we can cease the struggle, take the
light load Jesus offers us, and place all our other
burdens on him.

> **Falling used to mean we couldn't
> get up again; now we have
> a firm promise of a steady
> walk with God.**

*Though he stumble, he will not fall, for the Lord
upholds him with his hand.*   Psalm 37:24

The time will never come when we no longer
face temptation. Even Jesus was tempted,
though he never sinned. As long as we stay
under God's protection, submitting our life to
his control, we never need to fall again.

> Today is filled with trouble;
> tomorrow may be no better; but
> we have a promise from God—
> a bright forever.

*The righteous will inherit the land and dwell in
it forever.*   Psalm 37:29

Choosing to do right is the part we can do;
God has promised to do the rest. Those who
commit themselves to his care and submit to his
control God considers his children. Today, as
sons and daughters of God, all the benefits of
heaven belong to us.

> **Every day used to fill us with
> fear; now that God has taken
> control, fear of failure is gone.**

*To him who is able to keep you from falling and
to present you before his glorious presence without fault and with great joy—to the only God
our Savior be glory, majesty, power and authority, through Jesus Christ our Lord.*   Jude 24-25

When we admitted we were powerless over the
sins that entrapped us, we were suffering defeat
after defeat. Confidence was gone; self-esteem
was a forgotten dream. Now that recovery is
underway, we tend to hold on to our fears that
we will stumble and fall again. God promises
today that as long as we are under his control,
we have no need to fear.

Part Nine

Looking Better to Ourselves

The Lord your God is with you, he is mighty to save. He will take great delight in you, he will quiet you with his love, he will rejoice over you with singing.   Zephaniah 3:17

> **God wants us to have success;**
> **obeying him is the only way**
> **to achieve it.**

All these blessings will come upon you and accompany you if you obey the Lord your God: You will be blessed in the city and blessed in the country. The fruit of your womb will be blessed, and the crops of your land and the young of your livestock. Deuteronomy 28:2-4

No matter how badly we have failed in the past, there is hope for us today. As soon as we fully turn our life and will over to God and, through the strength he gives us, seek to obey him, the sooner we will turn a record of failure into success.

9 / 1

> No greater measure of success
> can be found than the smile
> of God upon us.

Then the Lord your God will make you most prosperous in all the work of your hands and in the fruit of your womb, the young of your livestock and the crops of your land. The Lord will again delight in you and make you prosperous, just as he delighted in your fathers.

Deuteronomy 30:9

We may have failed in the past because we failed to get the acclaim we thought we deserved from the world. The problem may have been that we sought the praise of men rather than the smile of God. Today we can make the heart of God glad by committing ourselves to pleasing him.

> **When we please God by the way
> we live, we can expect his
> blessing on us.**

*You will eat the fruit of your labor; blessings and
prosperity will be yours.*   Psalm 128:2

Successful people know that worthwhile goals
aren't achieved overnight. Bad habits caused
us, among other things, to lose the ability to post-
pone pleasure. Obedience to God is not a once-
for-all act; it calls for daily decisions to endure,
with God's help, some discomfort or pain until
the goal of full recovery is achieved.

The way to blessing is the path of obedience.

Therefore this is what the Sovereign Lord says:
"My servants will eat, but you will go hungry;
my servants will drink, but you will go thirsty;
my servants will rejoice, but you will be put to
shame. My servants will sing out of the joy of
their hearts, but you will cry out from anguish of
heart and wail in brokenness of spirit."

Isaiah 65:13-14

The decision to commit our life and will to God
made a profound difference only eternity can
fully explain, as that decision transformed us
from enemies to friends of God. Today, let us
live as God's friends and enjoy his fellowship.

> **Making obedience to God our
> chief goal assures us that
> God will make our prosperity
> his undertaking.**

*The Lord will grant you abundant prosperity—
in the fruit of your womb, the young of your livestock and the crops of your ground—in the land
he swore to your forefathers to give you. . . . If
you pay attention to the commands of the Lord
your God that I give you this day and carefully
follow them, you will always be at the top, never
at the bottom.*   Deuteronomy 28:11, 13

God is good. All through the Bible we see evi-
dences that he wants to enrich our life. Today
we can allow him to do so as we turn our life and
will over to him.

> **Recovery means a return to
> responsibility and hard work—
> and with God's blessing.**

*He who works his land will have abundant food,
but he who chases fantasies lacks judgment.*
                                        Proverbs 12:11

In the past, as sin clouded our minds, we often
hoped vainly that somehow things would get
better. But nothing changed. The difference
between a pipe dream and a goal is that a goal is
based on a plan to work toward its achievement.
God wants us to cooperate with him by doing
what we can.

Seeking God's will and wisdom is
the way to success—in this life
and the next.

---

*The teaching of the wise is a fountain of life,
turning a man from the snares of death.*

Proverbs 13:14

God has given clear instruction for our success. First, we must realize we can't succeed
without his help; then we must accept his help
by turning our life and will over to his control
and following him wherever he leads. Knowing
God's will isn't enough. Today, we can take one
more step toward recovery as we put into practice the wisdom he has given us.

> **Work is not a curse—it is the way God has chosen to give us his best.**

The hardworking farmer should be the first to receive a share of the crops.   2 Timothy 2:6

Success is not an honor or benefit conferred; it is a victory gained, and it is usually earned through our diligence and persistence. The good news for us today is that God through Jesus Christ has paved the way to victory, making it possible for us to go forth in his strength and power to achieve full recovery.

> **It takes courage to admit
> we have done wrong; but God
> blesses us when we do.**

*He will teach the ways that are right and best to
those who humbly turn to him.*　　Psalm 25:9; TLB

Making direct amends to those we have
harmed is an act of courage. Sometimes we hold
back from approaching people we have offended,
fearing that they won't forgive us. We must
come to the point where we are willing to make
amends even if they don't ever choose to forgive
us. Today God wants us to be humble, for that is
the kind of person he wants to help.

> **Being meek does not mean being weak; it means being kind and self-controlled.**

Blessed are the meek, for they will inherit the earth.   Matthew 5:5

Meekness takes more courage and strength than audacity, impudence, or combativeness. The most powerful person who ever walked on earth was Jesus, who said of himself that he was "gentle and humble in heart" (Matthew 11:29). Admitting our failures is difficult, but it is the best step we can take today toward finding wholeness.

> **Recovery comes from God;
> we make a big mistake when we
> take the credit for what God
> has done for us.**

*"Let him who boasts boast in the Lord." For
it is not the one who commends himself who is
approved, but the one whom the Lord commends.*   2 Corinthians 10:17-18

The good news we have to carry to others is
about God's work of recovery in our life. The
message must always be about what God has
done, and not about our own achievements.
Today, we must share the news with others in
great humility, as poor, hungry persons telling
other poor, hungry persons where we found
food.

> **Proud, haughty people who want
> more out of life than they are
> willing to give will never receive
> God's blessing.**

*Evil men do not understand justice, but those
who seek the Lord understand it fully. Better a
poor man whose walk is blameless than a rich
man whose ways are perverse.*   Proverbs 28:5-6

People of the world take pride in being powerful, overbearing, and domineering based on
their wealth or position of power. God measures
greatness in another way. Only the humble, the
meek, and the gentle experience God's blessing.
Today, as we seek to follow Christ, we must
remember that dealing justly and kindly with
others is the way to find God's presence and
blessing.

> **Pride kept us from admitting
> we had a problem; humility
> brought us to God, who was then
> able to help us.**

*The Lord sustains the humble but casts the
wicked to the ground.*   Psalm 147:6

As we daily examine our life and deal with the
wrongs we have done, we are insuring God's
blessing and protection. The proud ones, who
are unwilling to admit their sins, are bound to
fail. God's bright promise to us today is that as
we stay humble before him, he will sustain us,
protect us, and bless us with his presence.

> Humble, gentle people will
> always find favor with God.

A gentle answer turns away wrath, but a harsh word stirs up anger. Proverbs 15:1

People who raise their voices in anger are usually trying to defend themselves or justify their bad behavior. When God helps us to open up our heart, admit our failures, and seek to make restitution where possible, we may find we stir up old, deep-seated anger in others. God promises to bless our gentle answers, and today he wants to give us the grace and power to be gracious at such a difficult time.

> **To be proud is to claim credit for
> what God has done.**

*"Has not my hand made all these things, and so
they came into being?" declares the Lord. "This
is the one I esteem: he who is humble and con-
trite in spirit, and trembles at my word."*

Isaiah 66:2

Someone said that there is no limit to what
can be accomplished by people working together
when no one is concerned about who gets the
credit. We realize how true this is when we
consider what God has done for us as we have
cooperated with him in our recovery. God looks
with high favor on the person who doesn't brag
about his accomplishments, but acknowledges
God's help.

> **Sin and loss of control of our life
> made us see ourselves as
> worthless, but God considers us
> to be of great value.**

*So God created man in his own image, in the
image of God he created him; male and female
he created them.*   Genesis 1:27

Being created in God's image means we have
qualities and attributes like his. Nothing God
created should be considered worthless. No matter how much damage we have done, God still
sees us as redeemable. When we turn our life
over to him, he can continue his work of making
us like himself.

**We need to make certain that
we are judging ourselves as
God does.**

---

*But the Lord said to Samuel, "Do not consider
his appearance or his height, for I have rejected
him. The Lord does not look at the things man
looks at. Man looks at the outward appearance,
but the Lord looks at the heart."* 1 Samuel 16:7

We don't have eyes to see ourselves as God
does. We tend to measure ourselves by the way
the people of the world estimate themselves. God
sees our heart, understands our thoughts, and
determines quality by heavenly standards. As
we seek to know him better through his Word,
we become wiser and better able to evaluate
personal qualities.

❦

> **The world may see us as dirt, but**
> **God sees us as jewels.**

The Lord their God will save them on that day
as the flock of his people. They will sparkle in
his land like jewels in a crown. How attractive
and beautiful they will be! Grain will make the
young men thrive, and new wine the young
women. Zechariah 9:16-17

As we continue to take an inventory of our
life, we may think there is no end to the list of
people we have hurt and sins we have committed. Rather than think of the long list as an indication of how bad we are, we should consider
each failure we deal with as one step further
toward becoming the polished jewel of a person
God wants us to be.

> **Inner beauty character is
> far superior to outer adornment
> reputation!**

*Your beauty should not come from outward
adornment, such as braided hair and the wear-
ing of gold jewelry and fine clothes. Instead, it
should be that of your inner self, the unfading
beauty of a gentle and quiet spirit, which is of
great worth in God's sight.*   1 Peter 3:3-4

People spend millions on clothes and cosmetics
to improve their appearance. Those in public
office sometimes spend millions to improve their
image. God looks for inner beauty, which he can
give us today as we submit to his will and seek to
walk with him.

> We should never think of
> ourselves as worthless failures as
> long as God sees us as a part of
> his beautiful creation.

He has made everything beautiful in its time. He has also set eternity in the hearts of men; yet they cannot fathom what God has done from beginning to end.   Ecclesiastes 3:11

The more we learn about God through his Word, the more we learn about ourselves. The world may give us one impression of who we are, but God's evaluation is the only one that counts. We can be certain today, as we seek to live up to the truth God is giving us, that he is pleased with us.

> **A right relationship to God
> makes us beautiful in his eyes.**

*Charm is deceptive, and beauty is fleeting; but a
woman who fears the Lord is to be praised.*
Proverbs 31:30

Though this passage speaks of womanhood,
the truth is clear that anyone who puts God
first in his or her life will be considered praiseworthy, both in this world and in the courts of
heaven. God's promise for us today is that he
honors those who reverence him.

> Sin brought us self-hatred;
> it is only as we gain God's
> perspective on our recovery that
> we can see ourselves as delightful
> in his eyes.

For the Lord takes delight in his people; he crowns the humble with salvation.　　Psalm 149:4

Every sin, every failure, every offense we bring before God he will forgive; God will also help us as we seek to make amends to those we have harmed. God delights in such humility on our part. Today we find his mercy and grace available to us as we humble ourselves before him and others.

❧

Recognition of our spiritual need
is not highly esteemed by the
world, but it brings praise to God.

The poor will eat and be satisfied; they who seek the Lord will praise him. Psalm 22:26

God left us in the world for a purpose. Even those of us who have failed so often and allowed our life to become entrapped by sin can still fulfill God's purposes. As we allow him to deliver us from our sins and as we share the good news with others, we become examples of God's grace and cause others to praise him.

> When we lost control of our life,
> we may have inflicted severe
> damage on our body—
> but a gracious God can help us
> recover even our health.

If you listen carefully to the voice of the Lord your God and do what is right in his eyes, if you pay attention to his commands and keep all his decrees, I will not bring on you any of the diseases I brought on the Egyptians, for I am the Lord, who heals you. Exodus 15:26

Though God may have forgiven our sins, sometimes the consequences remain with us. Yet we can thank God that he is able, as he chooses, to restore us—body, soul, and spirit. We can trust him to make us all that he wants us to be.

> Turning our life over to God was
> the best thing we could have
> done—for our body, soul,
> and spirit.

*The Lord will guide you always; he will satisfy
your needs in a sun-scorched land and will
strengthen your frame. You will be like a well-
watered garden, like a spring whose waters
never fail.*   Isaiah 58:11

Sometimes during recovery, the part of us that
at the moment seems weakest—our body, soul,
or spirit—is the part we most need to rely on
during a hard time. Certainly God cares about
our total being—the physical frame as well, for
it is the temporary residence of the soul and
spirit. Today, we should trust God to restore to
us the health, physical or emotional, that we
need to please him. He can do it!

> **The best thing to do for our
> wounded life is to bring it to
> Jesus for his healing touch.**

*When evening came, many who were demon-pos-
sessed were brought to him, and he drove out the
spirits with a word and healed all the sick. This
was to fulfill what was spoken through the
prophet Isaiah: "He took up our infirmities and
carried our diseases."*   Matthew 8:16-17

When we are discouraged, we bring our
wounded heart to Jesus; when we feel spiritually
exhausted, we ask for a renewal of spirit. God
today may want to encourage you by touching
your physical body. Trust him to give you all
you need for today.

Sin weakens and destroys; our
trust in Jesus Christ can bring
healing to our soul.

*By faith in the name of Jesus, this man whom
you see and know was made strong. It is Jesus'
name and the faith that comes through him that
has given this complete healing to him, as you
can all see.* Acts 3:16

God used physical healing to demonstrate
what he can do in the spiritual realm. Today we
may feel the need of such encouragement from
him. God remembers us, how ill or well we are,
and he cares. We must trust him today for all of
our needs.

> **Sin took years from our life;
> submitting to God's control can
> restore some of those years.**

*Even to your old age and gray hairs I am he, I
am he who will sustain you. I have made you
and I will carry you; I will sustain you and I will
rescue you.*   Isaiah 46:4

Many of the things we suffered in the body
will trouble us the rest of our life on earth. But
many of the lessons we learned from the pain,
and the enriched life we now enjoy as a result,
give us a better perspective on eternity. Long life
is a blessing, given by God to extend our usefulness to him here on earth. May we use our life
wisely for him today.

> **Physical addiction, like spiritual
> entrapment, needs God's
> healing touch.**

*And the prayer offered in faith will make the
sick person well; the Lord will raise him up. If
he has sinned, he will be forgiven.*   James 5:15

Physical healing and spiritual healing from
the deadly effects of sin are often spoken of
together, as in this promise. God's promise for
forgiveness of sin remains one of the most pre-
cious gifts he has given us. Let us trust him
today to keep us healthy—spiritually and physically.

> **The basis for our recovery is
> God's mercy, bought for us by
> Christ on the cross.**

*He himself bore our sins in his body on the tree,
so that we might die to sins and live for righteousness; by his wounds you have been healed.*
1 Peter 2:24

We are mortal; death will one day overtake us all, and some of us will, in God's perfect plan, exit from this life into the glories of the life to come through the veil of some of the sicknesses and diseases common to the world today. But one promise of God is certain; the disease of sin has found a cure in the cross of Christ. Today we can thank God that our spirit has found eternal healing in Christ.

Part Ten

Dealing with Temptation

*The Lord can rescue you and
me from the temptations that
surround us.* 2 Peter 2:9; TLB

Once God has control of our life,
he wants us to learn
self-control—the ability to say
yes to good and no to evil.

*How can a young man keep his way pure? By
living according to your word. I seek you with
all my heart; do not let me stray from your
commands.*　　　　　　　　　Psalm 119:9-10

The best way to keep saying no to the things
that nearly destroyed us is to keep our relationship with God clear through prayer and meditation on his Word. Today we dare not face the
world without a sense of his presence.

> **We say no to sin through the
> power God has given us.**

*I pray also that the eyes of your heart may be
enlightened in order that you may know the
hope to which he has called you, the riches of his
glorious inheritance in the saints, and his incom-
parably great power for us who believe. That
power is like the working of his mighty strength,
which he exerted in Christ when he raised him
from the dead and seated him at his right hand
in the heavenly realms.*   Ephesians 1:18-20

Only eternity will tell us how much we have in
Christ that became ours through his death and
resurrection. His power is enough to help us say
no to any temptation that may come our way
today.

> **The one who stands beside us in
> our temptation has faced
> temptation victoriously,
> so he knows how to make
> us victors.**

*Therefore, since we have a great high priest who
has gone through the heavens, Jesus the Son of
God, let us hold firmly to the faith we profess.
For we do not have a high priest who is unable
to sympathize with our weaknesses, but we have
one who has been tempted in every way, just as
we are—yet was without sin.*

Hebrews 4:14-15

We may think no one understands just how
powerful the temptations are. God provided an
answer for us when he gave us the example of
Jesus, who knows about temptation. Because
he faced it victoriously, he is able to take us
through any enticement the evil one may send
at us today.

> **The future is bright for those
> who allow God to support them
> during testing.**

*Blessed is the man who perseveres under trial,
because when he has stood the test, he will
receive the crown of life that God has promised
to those who love him.*   James 1:12

If we were not tested, we would never know
just how weak we are and how strong God is to
deliver us from temptation. We will never be
strong in our own power. God knows how much
testing we can take. He gives us for today all the
strength we need to face anything he will allow
to come upon us.

> God allows temptation, but
> he does not originate it. He does,
> however, use it to show
> how powerful he is to help
> us be overcomers.

*When tempted, no one should say, "God is tempt-
ing me." For God cannot be tempted by evil, nor
does he tempt anyone.*   James 1:13

God didn't originate evil. The evil that comes
our way is a result of a world that turned its
back on God. God's work is redemption—
buying us back from the power of sin. We
should remember today when temptation comes
that God is at our side to help us say no to sin
and yes to righteousness.

> **We cannot say no to the evil one
> unless we say yes to God.**

*Submit yourselves, then, to God. Resist the
devil, and he will flee from you. Come near to
God and he will come near to you.*   James 4:7-8

In the past we thought we could control our
life. Then we became entrapped and realized we
were wrong. The decision we made to believe
God could help us was a wise one, for it opened
the way for God to strengthen us. Today, we
should thank God that he is available to help us
say no to temptation.

God wants to make us
victors today.

---

*May our Lord Jesus Christ himself and God our
Father, who loved us and by his grace gave us
eternal encouragement and good hope, encourage your hearts and strengthen you in every
good deed and word.*   2 Thessalonians 2:16-17

The God we serve wants to be known as both
holy and loving. Because he is holy, he must deal
with our sin. Because he is loving, he wants to
help us be all we should be. Today, we should
be encouraged to know that all the power of God
is available to make us strong to make good
choices.

> **Turning away from sin and sinful
> people may put us on a lonely
> road. But we are not alone—
> God walks with us.**

*I am with you and will watch over you wherever
you go, and I will bring you back to this land. I
will not leave you until I have done what I have
promised you."*   Genesis 28:15

Staying free from sin means saying good-bye to
a lot of people with whom we once shared a life-
style of sin. Sometimes the pain of loneliness can
seem very intense until we form new, more
wholesome friendships. Perhaps God will, in
time, give us a new family of friends; but in the
meantime he wants us to know he is a friend who
never leaves us. We need to remember that
today.

> **Sin separates us from good
> people; drawing close
> to God makes us members of
> a new family.**

*God sets the lonely in families, he leads forth the
prisoners with singing; but the rebellious live in
a sun-scorched land.*　　　　Psalm 68:6

We needed the help of others when we were
struggling to break the old habits. As we grow
stronger others will need our help. The fellowship of recovering people, drawn together by
God's grace, can mean as much to us as any
physical, earthly family. Today, God wants us
to enjoy our fellowship with him and his other
children. They are one of the many good gifts
God has given us.

As the bride of Christ, we need
never feel lonely or unloved.

*For your Maker is your husband—the Lord
Almighty is his name—the Holy One of Israel is
your Redeemer; he is called the God of all the
earth.*   Isaiah 54:5

God used the picture of a husband and wife
to illustrate the intimate and loving relationship
he wants to have with us. How much love and
desire to protect and nurture does a bridegroom
feel for his bride? It would be just the smallest
picture of how God loves you today.

10 / 10

> **People of the world reject us**
> **when we fail them; God loves us**
> **and brings us back, no matter**
> **how far we stray from him.**

I will betroth you to me forever; I will betroth
you in righteousness and justice, in love and
compassion.
Hosea 2:19

One certainty about human relationships is
that they will all fail in time. Sin, hatred, or
death will end every one of them. But God has
called us to a forever relationship. To be lonely
is to misunderstand just how close and intimate
God wants to be with us. Today we should seek
to know him better so we can be forever delivered from the fear of loneliness.

Turning our life over to God may
seem like a leap into the dark.
Today's promise shines light
on that decision.

*The Lord your God is with you, he is mighty to
save. He will take great delight in you, he will
quiet you with his love, he will rejoice over you
with singing."* Zephaniah 3:17

Saying good-bye to the past way of life may
have given us the feeling we were facing a long,
lonely road. Learning a new way of life does
seem a hollow existence for a while. But God
wants us to know that he wants to be all we
need: a friend, a provider, and a comforter. We
need to cast ourselves into his arms today and
let him love us.

> ## The cure for today's empty
> ## feeling is God's fullness.

*You have been given fullness in Christ, who is the
head over every power and authority.*

Colossians 2:10

It may seem an empty promise to us, when we
feel a deep sense of loneliness, to say that Christ
wants to be our friend. Humanly speaking, we
often feel we need the warmth of another human
being, a friend to whom we can talk, someone
who can sympathize when we feel overwhelmed
with temptation. While that may be the way we
feel, we should take God at his word today and
let him show us just how much he can make us
feel loved.

> ## No one needs to feel alienated from God.

Come near to God and he will come near to you.
James 4:8

When we seek to know God better through prayer and study of his Word, we grow in knowledge about him. More than just knowing *about* him, we come to know *him*. He never forces himself on us, but he always loves us. He is always as near to us, in time of joy or sorrow, as we want him to be.

Old friends—sometimes even
families—abandon us in our
distress; but when we need help
the most, God offers to adopt
us as his very own child.

*I will not leave you as orphans; I will come to
you.*
                                            John 14:18

The alienation brought about by our past
failures and the sense of loneliness and aban-
donment can be painful. One bright promise
remains for us today. When we turn our life and
will over to God, he takes us into his family. We
never have to feel like an orphan again as long
as we have a loving heavenly Father.

Help is as close and available as
God, who is always near.

The righteous cry out, and the Lord hears them;
he delivers them from all their troubles.

Psalm 34:17

"Once burned, twice careful," we say. Fear of
another failure can stymie our progress and pre-
vent us from moving out in trust that God can
keep us. It is true that we should avoid the situations that caused us to fail, but we must believe
God can give us strength and courage to live
again, knowing that he is ready to help us when
overpowering temptations return.

❧

> **Adam and Eve, Jesus, and every
> one of us have faced and will
> face temptation. God's concern is
> in *how* we face it.**

*No temptation has seized you except what is
common to man. And God is faithful; he will not
let you be tempted beyond what you can bear.
But when you are tempted, he will also provide
a way out so that you can stand up under it.*
                                    1 Corinthians 10:13

Today we have this bright promise from God:
that he knows and understands what we are facing. He knows what we can bear; he will never
put us in waters too deep or fires too hot for us.
Somewhere in our dark, anguish-filled cave,
there is a ray of light that points to an escape
passage.

> **Calling on God is an admission of our powerlessness; God honors our cry for help with all of his power.**

Call upon me in the day of trouble; I will deliver you, and you will honor me."   Psalm 50:15

Healing was kept from us during those days when we were too proud to admit that we were out of control. When we submitted our life and will to God, he began a healing work that continues as long as we stay dependent upon him. God's ear is open to our cry for help all day, every day—especially today.

> The power of evil has been
> broken; we can march in the
> victory parade today.

*He who does what is sinful is of the devil,
because the devil has been sinning from the
beginning. The reason the Son of God appeared
was to destroy the devil's work.* 1 John 3:8

There was a time when we had to admit we had
lost control over the addicting and debilitating
sins that nearly destroyed us. But once we
turned our life over to God for his care and
control, we can resist Satan's power to control
us by entering into the victory Christ won for us.

> **We may not see the way out
> today—but God does!**

*The Lord knows how to rescue godly men from
trials and to hold the unrighteous for the day of
judgment, while continuing their punishment.*
                                                2 Peter 2:9

Our Creator knows all about us and the parts
of our past that nearly destroyed us. He knows
all about those who would continue to influence
us toward evil. God wants us to be comfortable
in his presence today, and he wants us to be
assured that he can deliver us from any temptation we want to escape.

> **Others mistakenly say they understand when we are tempted—but Jesus really does!**

For we do not have a high priest who is unable to sympathize with our weaknesses, but we have one who has been tempted in every way, just as we are—yet was without sin. Let us then approach the throne of grace with confidence, so that we may receive mercy and find grace to help us in our time of need. Hebrews 4:15-16

When temptations come today, we can rely on the one who knows how to overcome and how to make us overcome.

> **We no longer have to act like dead, powerless people—God has made us alive!**

All of us also lived among them at one time, gratifying the cravings of our sinful nature and following its desires and thoughts. Like the rest, we were by nature objects of wrath. But because of his great love for us, God, who is rich in mercy, made us alive with Christ even when we were dead in transgressions—it is by grace you have been saved.
Ephesians 2:3-5

Spiritual life has been given us; today we have an obligation both to live responsibly and to share the Good News of life with others.

> The Good Shepherd, who passed
> through the valley of shadows
> himself, knows how to lead us.

*Because he himself suffered when he was
tempted, he is able to help those who are being
tempted.*   Hebrews 2:18

Unsympathetic onlookers can be of little help
to us who are recovering from a shameful past.
"I know what you're going through," they say,
but rarely do they really know. But when we see
what Jesus endured, and how he emerged victorious, his words of hope, challenge, and promise
of help really mean something.

> **Former friends may now be considered enemies, now that God has been given control of our life.**

But I will rescue you on that day, declares the Lord; you will not be handed over to those you fear. I will save you; you will not fall by the sword but will escape with your life, because you trust in me, declares the Lord.   Jeremiah 39:17-18

Old temptations, whether they come in the form of a substance or a person, must be treated now as enemies of our soul. God wants us to love our human enemies, but we must not allow these old friendships to drag us down again. Maintaining our relationship with God through prayer and meditation on his Word is our best defense.

> God wants to lead us today in
> paths of righteousness, even as
> our old enemies look on.

*He will call upon me, and I will answer him; I
will be with him in trouble, I will deliver him and
honor him.* Psalm 91:15

Those who used to take part with us in the
sinful way of life that entrapped us may be looking on, waiting for us to fall. Our changed life
makes them uncomfortable, and some even
plot our downfall. We can take courage today,
remembering that God's ear is always attentive
to hear our cry for help.

> **The best way to face an enemy is
> with a Friend at our side.**

*People of Zion, who live in Jerusalem, you will
weep no more. How gracious he will be when
you cry for help! As soon as he hears, he will
answer you.* Isaiah 30:19

The time will never come on earth when we
have no difficulties to face. With good reason
earth is often called a "vale of tears." The hope
we have today is that we have a God who offers
us comfort for our tears, courage for our fears,
and the covenant promise of his presence
throughout the day.

> **Our unseen resources, God's
> presence and power, are more
> than enough for today.**

*"Don't be afraid," the prophet answered.
"Those who are with us are more than those
who are with them."*   2 Kings 6:16

Only those who become acquainted with God
through his Word have eyes to see the powerful
host surrounding us with protection. When we
turn our life over to God for his care, we can be
sure his shield is between us and any attacks by
our enemies.

> **Overcomers leave defensive
> positions and put their enemies
> to flight.**

*The Lord will grant that the enemies who rise up
against you will be defeated before you. They
will come at you from one direction but flee from
you in seven.*   Deuteronomy 28:7

There is a time to defend our positions, to
ward off the attacks of temptation. There is
also a time to count on God to help us put the
enemy on the run. A good way to begin defeating
the enemy is by dealing with our past failures,
making restitution, and proceeding on to greater
victories with a clean heart and a clear conscience.

> **Submission to and worship of
> God put him on our side to fight
> against the enemy.**

*Rather, worship the Lord your God; it is he who
will deliver you from the hand of all your enemies."*   2 Kings 17:39

Rebellion against God was the beginning of
our problems. Unless God is in control of our
life, someone or something else soon takes control. Only as we cease from our rebellion and
turn our life and will over to God do we begin
to realize victory over the enemies that were
destroying us.

> **If we love God, we will hate the things that he hates.**

Let those who love the Lord hate evil, for he guards the lives of his faithful ones and delivers them from the hand of the wicked. Psalm 97:10

As long as we held on to our sinful habits, refusing God's help, we were on our own against the enemy. Once we surrendered our life to him, he became our best friend and our best protector. Today, thank God that he is on guard over our soul.

Part Eleven

Living with the Consequences

*"Comfort, yes, comfort my
people," says your God.
"Speak tenderly to Jerusalem
and tell her that her sad days
are gone. Her sins are par-
doned, and I have punished
her in full for all her sins."*

Isaiah 40:1-2; TLB

> **After taking many wrong steps,
> we must learn the hard way how
> to stay on the right path.**

Blessed is the man whom God corrects; so do not despise the discipline of the Almighty. For he wounds, but he also binds up; he injures, but his hands also heal. Job 5:17-18

"No pain, no gain," we say. Some of the pain we suffer is from the open wounds or the scars of past sins. Sometimes the pain comes from withdrawal—like the excruciating experience of pulling a deeply embedded thorn, always a traumatic experience. For whatever reason, God allows it. He intends it to make us better people. If God didn't love us, he would leave us in our deadly trap.

> **Reward and punishment,
> pleasure and pain, are the
> universal tools of discipline; God
> knows how to use both.**

*Blessed is the man you discipline, O Lord, the
man you teach from your law; you grant him
relief from days of trouble, till a pit is dug for
the wicked.*   Psalm 94:12-13

One of the most serious forms of child abuse
is neglect—allowing a child to continue in bad
habits and undisciplined behavior. A loving
heavenly Father knows what we need, even
when it is discipline. We should thank God
today that his guiding hand is on us, turning us
toward the right way.

11 / 2

**Submission to God's discipline
is his way of bringing us
to full maturity.**

*My son, do not despise the Lord's discipline and
do not resent his rebuke, because the Lord disciplines those he loves, as a father the son he
delights in.*   Proverbs 3:11-12

Sometimes the shaping tools of the wood-
carver seem severe, but the finished workman-
ship brings praise to the craftsman. If we
weren't loved so much, such effort would not
be expended on us. The pain is to shape our life
so that we bring delight to our Creator and
Redeemer and become an example to others of
what God can do to a life that is submitted to
his discipline.

Rebellion against wise authority
is the beginning of most
addictions.

A fool spurns his father's discipline, but whoever heeds correction shows prudence.   Proverbs 15:5

When we refuse God-given authority over us, we invite other powers to take control of our life. Once we have lost control, we are at the mercy of the evil one. Only as we turn our life and will over to God and accept his discipline, as a son accepts the discipline of his father, can we find help in breaking the old habits. God's promise for today is that he offers freedom to us as we put our life under his control.

> **God promises to spare us judgment if we enter his disciplinary training.**

When we are judged by the Lord, we are being disciplined so that we will not be condemned with the world.   1 Corinthians 11:32

There is a colossal difference between corrective discipline and punitive judgment. Sometimes in our immature thinking we confuse the two. God brings restraints into our life to keep us from the deeper chasm of eternal punishment. Today we should thank God that he cares enough about us to discipline us as a loving father, rather than punish us as a righteous judge.

> **While we discipline sometimes in anger, God disciplines in love.**

The Lord disciplines those he loves, and he pun-ishes everyone he accepts as a son. . . . Our fathers disciplined us for a little while as they thought best; but God disciplines us for our good, that we may share in his holiness.

Hebrews 12:6, 10

Getting to know God through his Word and prayer makes us more aware of what he desires for us. The more we know of his will, the more he holds us responsible to obey. If we don't grow from what we learn we do damage to our spirit. God in love helps us to grow more and more like himself. Thank him today for all he does to keep us walking in his ways.

> Every ache we feel during our
> recovery provides an occasion to
> become stronger.

*But those who suffer he delivers in their suffer-
ing; he speaks to them in their affliction.*

Job 36:15

Many diseases we suffer develop within our
body an immunity that makes us stronger to
stand against other similar diseases. The pain
we are willing to endure to recover, with God's
help, can make us stronger and less susceptible
to falling into the same sins again. Today God
wants to turn our suffering into strength, and he
will as we allow him to do so.

> **Following God is often like a
> rock-strewn path, but he guides
> us safely all the way.**

*This is what the Lord says—your Redeemer, the
Holy One of Israel: "I am the Lord your God,
who teaches you what is best for you, who
directs you in the way you should go."*

Isaiah 48:17

Following God is not easy; sometimes he calls
us through a desert in order to bring us to a
promised land of blessing. Turning our life over
to him, learning to say no to the sins that kept us
in subjection, always pulls against the easy way
our flesh longs to go. But recovery is in sight,
and the pleasure of his presence along the way
makes today's struggles worthwhile.

> **Even spiritually, we must learn to
> walk before we run.**

*Do not gloat over me, my enemy! Though I have
fallen, I will rise. Though I sit in darkness, the
Lord will be my light. Because I have sinned
against him, I will bear the Lord's wrath, until
he pleads my case and establishes my right. He
will bring me out into the light; I will see his righteousness.*   Micah 7:8-9

Past sins and rebellions have taken a toll, and
some of their consequences may plague us for a
while yet. But even this struggle is part of the
growth process through which our loving God
allows us to pass to make us strong.

❧

> **Real progress is best measured in terms of our long-range goals.**

Therefore we do not lose heart. Though outwardly we are wasting away, yet inwardly we are being renewed day by day. For our light and momentary troubles are achieving for us an eternal glory that far outweighs them all.

2 Corinthians 4:16-17

When the pull of temptation is on us and we feel weakest in resolve, we can thank God for his presence to see us through. Sometimes it may seem the pressure will never let up; yet we know God is using these times to make us better people, more like him, and more useful to the world around us when his perfecting work in us is done.

> **Discouragement is not of God;
> it comes from the enemy, who is
> trying to divert us from the
> right path.**

*Why are you downcast, O my soul? Why so
disturbed within me? Put your hope in God, for
I will yet praise him, my Savior and my God.*
                                        Psalm 42:11

All through the Scriptures men and women
faced dark days, with discouraging attacks coming from all sides. Yet, never do we see God
using discouragement as an instrument to fulfill
his purpose. We can be certain at such times
that God wants us to look up, take fresh courage, and celebrate another day in his presence,
counting on his power.

God wants us to face up to our
troublesome past so he can
forgive it and help us
overcome it.

*Though you have made me see troubles, many
and bitter, you will restore my life again; from
the depths of the earth you will again bring me
up.*   Psalm 71:20

Making amends for the past brings back to us
and to the ones we have offended many bad
memories. Like an old infection, some of these
old wounds to the soul don't get better until they
are opened and cleansed so healing can begin
from within. Jesus is the Great Physician, who
can bring healing to any of these injured relationships. He wants us to trust him to do that
for us today.

11 / 12

Recovery is working with God to rebuild our broken life.

"But now be strong . . . ," declares the Lord.
"Be strong . . . all you people of the land . . .
and work. For I am with you," declares the
Lord Almighty.   Haggai 2:4

We tried in our own strength, and nothing
happened. We placed the blame on others—even
on God, but no recovery came. Then we turned
our life over to him and began to cooperate with
what he wanted to do in our life, and the healthy
changes began. Today God calls us to keep up
the good work, because he is with us.

> **God gives victories to those who want his help.**

The salvation of the righteous comes from the Lord; he is their stronghold in time of trouble. The Lord helps them and delivers them; he delivers them from the wicked and saves them, because they take refuge in him.   Psalm 37:39-40

Our efforts are important for our recovery, but too much self-confidence sometimes results in overconfidence and failure. Dependence on God doesn't mean we leave everything up to him. God responds willingly to our cries for help, but he doesn't force it on us. We should be grateful for his deliverance and trust him for all we need today.

Nothing is too hard for God to do for you today. Count on him!

He performs wonders that cannot be fathomed, miracles that cannot be counted.   Job 5:9

Sometimes the task of getting our life back on track, making amends for all the failures of the past, and struggling to develop a new life-style free from old habits seems too much. But we must remember that we have turned our life over to a powerful, miracle-working God, who wants to show himself strong on our behalf today.

❧

> The game isn't over yet; evil
> people seem to prosper, but God
> hasn't finished his work in us.

*Surely God does not reject a blameless man or
strengthen the hands of evildoers. He will yet fill
your mouth with laughter and your lips with
shouts of joy.* Job 8:20-21

Trying to compare ourselves with others,
who haven't faced the struggles we have to face
in recovery, can be discouraging. We need to
remember that God, to whom we have committed our life, is working in us so that one day we
can smile again. That is the hope we have to help
us through today's struggles.

11 / 16

> There is a place we can go to
> escape the pressure of
> temptation—God's presence.

*You are my hiding place; you will protect me
from trouble and surround me with songs of
deliverance.*   Psalm 32:7

Meditation on God's Word and prayer equip
us for today's battle with ourselves—the old tugs
toward a former life-style and toward making
bad choices again. God wants us to turn to him
today, to seek his protecting arms. He is a safe
place of refuge.

> **We must believe that God is far more willing to help us than we are willing to seek help.**

Call upon me in the day of trouble; I will deliver you, and you will honor me. Psalm 50:15

It takes the kind of eyes God can give us to see beyond ourselves, our own needs, and our own safety. We tend to forget that our good choices bring glory and praise to our Creator and Redeemer. Calling on him to help us in our crises is not a sign of weakness, but a sign of faith in a good, loving God. He wants to hear our cries for help today.

> **Learning to suffer is a part of
> learning to postpone pleasure
> until a more appropriate time.**

*Since you have kept my command to endure
patiently, I will also keep you from the hour of
trial that is going to come upon the whole world
to test those who live on the earth.*

Revelation 3:10

Jesus suffered on earth during his earthly min-
istry. By doing so he set us an example of how to
endure. As he was raised to glory when the
ordeal was over, so we shall be lifted up one day.
The joys we savor as we overcome the problems
that once defeated us are only a picture of the
eternal joys that await us in the future.

We will never know how strong is
the right hand of God until we
hold it in the night of adversity.

*Though I walk in the midst of trouble, you pre-
serve my life; you stretch out your hand against
the anger of my foes, with your right hand you
save me.*   Psalm 138:7

Those who have never suffered greatly may
never understand God's comfort. Those who
haven't faced severe temptation may not understand God's power to save. Learning to suffer
means learning to find God strong on our
behalf. During today's encounter with a hostile
world, we can count on his strong defense and
his loving presence.

> Sadness and adversity don't
> mean abandonment by God; they
> may be his means of building
> strength of character.

*The Lord gives sight to the blind, the Lord lifts
up those who are bowed down, the Lord loves
the righteous.*
                                        Psalm 146:8

We can't judge God's work by the way we feel
at this moment. Testing of our spirit, like strain-
ing muscles to the limit, sometimes builds our
spiritual life to be more useful to God in the
future. It may be dark, but God is light. We may
be bowed down now, but God loves us and will
lift us up if we will just trust him and keep our
eyes on him.

> **Enduring hardship for Christ
> today means we can be enjoying
> his victory tomorrow.**

*I have told you these things, so that in me you
may have peace. In this world you will have
trouble. But take heart! I have overcome the
world.*   John 16:33

It helps us to know that our Savior endured
hard moments here on earth. He has called us
into his fellowship and confidence, sharing these
words of comfort and encouragement. Today he
asks us to "Take heart." Instead of being overwhelmed, we can be an overcomer with him.

> **God offers all we need for
> today—every day.**

*For just as the sufferings of Christ flow over into
our lives, so also through Christ our comfort
overflows.*   2 Corinthians 1:5

It would be a cruel God who would ask us
to enter fires of suffering for which he himself
had no solace. Because God calls us to go
through hard times for our own good and for
his glory, he also provides all we need of comfort, strength, and patience to endure. Today
we can be grateful that he understands all that
we endure in our pilgrimage toward wholeness.

> Our cries in the darkness seem
> for a moment to go nowhere; but
> God hears and will respond at
> just the right moment.

For he has not despised or disdained the suffering of the afflicted one; he has not hidden his face from him but has listened to his cry for help.   Psalm 22:24

The world turns away from us during those times when our pain becomes too much for them to watch. But God is a friend who stays the long night with us. When we turned our life and will over to him, he assumed responsibility for our welfare. Today's problems can become stepping stones for new works of grace and restoration in our life.

> **Today's stumbling is temporary;**
> **final victory is assured.**

But if . . . you seek the Lord your God, you will find him if you look for him with all your heart and with all your soul. When you are in distress and all these things have happened to you, then in later days you will return to the Lord your God and obey him. For the Lord your God is a merciful God; he will not abandon or destroy you or forget the covenant with your forefathers, which he confirmed to them by oath.

Deuteronomy 4:29-31

Today is a new day to see God, and if the ears of our heart are turned clearly to his voice, good things can happen.

> No matter how far we have
> fallen, God is still ready
> to restore us.

*If my people, who are called by my name, will
humble themselves and pray and seek my face
and turn from their wicked ways, then will I
hear from heaven and will forgive their sin and
will heal their land.* 2 Chronicles 7:14

Sin takes a toll—on a nation, a people, and
individuals like us. Others may give up on us
when we fail, but God continues to hold out
hope for us; his promise to restore us remains
fresh and available.

> We rise from defeat when we
> start keeping the right company.

*Blessed is the man who does not walk in the
counsel of the wicked or stand in the way of sinners or sit in the seat of mockers. But his delight
is in the law of the Lord, and on his law he medi-
tates day and night.*　　　　　Psalm 1:1-2

The community of God's people is the safest
place for us to be when we are seeking to recover
from the effects of an addiction. God can't bless
us if we continue in the places we used to go,
keeping friendships with those who led us
astray. The best place to be is where God is—
with his people.

> **Wounded from the struggles of
> life, we need the healing
> God can give us.**

*He heals the brokenhearted and binds up their
wounds.*   Psalm 147:3

The world and its attractions made a slave of
us and left us wounded on the roadside of life.
Jesus found us, picked us up, and brought spiritual healing to the wounds sin had caused.
Today we must continue in that victory and healing he gave, thanking him for what he did for us
and staying on the winning side.

In the midst of failure, we have a
clear promise of rescue.

*"For I know the plans I have for you," declares
the Lord, "plans to prosper you and not to harm
you, plans to give you hope and a future. Then
you will call upon me and come and pray to me,
and I will listen to you. You will seek me and find
me when you seek me with all your heart."*
Jeremiah 29:11-13

When we are fighting to regain control of our
life, there may be many disappointing moments
when, in our weakness, we give in again to the
sinful practices that enslaved us before. Some
of the ways God leads during those times seem
hard and difficult to understand. But the wise
Creator is also the wise Shepherd who knows
how to lead us in the right direction.

> Patience—God hasn't
> forgotten us. Our life didn't get
> into trouble in a moment;
> recovery won't come
> suddenly either.

*The Lord is not slow in keeping his promise, as
some understand slowness. He is patient with
you, not wanting anyone to perish, but everyone
to come to repentance.* 2 Peter 3:9

In our desire to be free not only from the
effects of our former life-style, but also from
the temptations that seek to attract us back into
it, we grow impatient. We wonder if those who
caused us trouble will ever have to pay for their
part of the wrongdoing. But God is a promise-
keeping God. He will rescue us in his time, and
he will deal with evil in his own way. We can
trust him for that today—and every day.

Part Twelve

Thinking of Others

I want you to share your food with the hungry and bring right into your own homes those who are helpless, poor, and destitute. Clothe those who are cold, and don't hide from relatives who need your help. If you do these things, God will shed his own glorious light upon you. He will heal you; your godliness will lead you forward, goodness will be a shield before you, and the glory of the Lord will protect you from behind. Isaiah 58:7-8; TLB

**More important than any other
opinion is what God thinks of us.**

---

*Blessed are those who are persecuted because of
righteousness, for theirs is the kingdom of
heaven. Blessed are you when people insult you,
persecute you and falsely say all kinds of evil
against you because of me. Rejoice and be glad,
because great is your reward in heaven, for in
the same way they persecuted the prophets who
were before you.*   Matthew 5:10-12

Some of the criticism we face is caused by our
own wrongdoing, but often—especially when we
are turning our life toward God's ways—people
put pressure on us to return to our old ways.
Remember, God is on our side, as long as we are
on his.

> **The enemy doesn't like it when we challenge the hold he once had on us.**

For in the day of trouble he will keep me safe in his dwelling; he will hide me in the shelter of his tabernacle and set me high upon a rock. Then my head will be exalted above the enemies who surround me; at his tabernacle will I sacrifice with shouts of joy; I will sing and make music to the Lord.   Psalm 27:5-6

Attacks can come from many sources. Many things and people will conspire against us when we are trying to get free from the entrapment of sin. Remember today that God's protection is around us when we submit our life and will to him.

> **God understands us;**
> **we must worry more about what**
> **he thinks and less about what**
> **others say of us.**

*In the shelter of your presence you hide them
from the intrigues of men; in your dwelling you
keep them safe from accusing tongues.*

Psalm 31:20

Our worst attacks may come in the form of
ridicule from those who take our new stand
for right as superficial or a "holier than thou"
attitude. Some evil-minded people set their
minds to make us fall again. We must let God
be our protector today.

> **Turning toward God means
> turning from the world and
> worldly people, and sometimes
> they hate us for it.**

*He will send down help from heaven to save me
because of his love and his faithfulness. He will
rescue me from these liars who are so intent
upon destroying me.*   Psalm 57:3; TLB

Well-meaning people can hurt us by the things
they say—how much more are we hurt, then, by
those who intentionally try to ridicule us for our
stand for God. God is our defense; today we
must count on his encouragement and ignore
those who pursue us with their malicious words.

> If we defend ourselves, God
> won't; if we don't defend
> ourselves, God will.

A false witness will not go unpunished, and he who pours out lies will perish.   Proverbs 19:9

Harmful lies about us are hard to escape. Only God can turn around the falsehood others spread about us. Some of the hurtful things said about us result from rightful criticism of our former behavior. But if we are looking to God for protection, he will see that the harm done will not be permanent. If we take care of our character, God will take care of our reputation.

> **Suffering for Christ's sake can prove to be the source of great blessing.**

If you are insulted because of the name of Christ, you are blessed, for the Spirit of glory and of God rests on you.   1 Peter 4:14

God does not take lightly the insults heaped on his children. He hasn't forgotten those who heaped shameful abuse on his Son, and he won't forget those who insult us in Jesus' name. Today we have good reason to feel sorry for those who attack our stand for righteousness, knowing God honors us when we endure it patiently.

> God hasn't promised a life
> without trouble; what he
> promised is a life without fear.

Who is going to harm you if you are eager to do good? But even if you should suffer for what is right, you are blessed. "Do not fear what they fear; do not be frightened." 1 Peter 3:13-14

It is true that harm can come to us, even as we try to break old habits and walk in God's ways. But we are promised God's presence today, so we don't have to fear because God is near and rewards those who are eager to please him.

> **Next to God, our family must
> take a high place in our heart.**

*Children, obey your parents in the Lord, for this
is right. "Honor your father and mother"—
which is the first commandment with a promise—"that it may go well with you and that you
may enjoy long life on the earth."*

Ephesians 6:1-3

God, wanting to show us more clearly what
our relationship to him should be, instituted the
family as an object lesson of the love between a
father and his children. Our relationships to our
earthly father and to our heavenly Father often
parallel. Today, God's blessing is on those who
make family life a priority.

> As God blesses us, our family will
> be enriched also.

*For I will pour water on the thirsty land, and
streams on the dry ground; I will pour out my
Spirit on your offspring, and my blessing on
your descendants.*   Isaiah 44:3

The best thing we can do to restore our family
is to allow God to make us all we can be. Today,
accept God's promise to pour the fresh water of
the Spirit into your life, that it may overflow to
a family that needs you.

> **Godly parents encourage their
> family to also please their
> heavenly Father.**

---

*The father of a righteous man has great joy; he
who has a wise son delights in him. May your
father and mother be glad; may she who gave
you birth rejoice! My son, give me your heart
and let your eyes keep to my ways.*

Proverbs 23:24-26

So much of how we behave in life relates to our
family life. God promises to bless fathers and
mothers today as they honor him in their homes.
In turn, their children, blessed by godly parents, will walk in obedience, bringing glory to
both their parents and their heavenly Father.

> We are more important to our
> children's spiritual health than
> we may realize.

*We will tell the next generation the praiseworthy
deeds of the Lord, his power, and the wonders
he has done. He decreed statutes . . . which
he commanded our forefathers to teach their
children, so the next generation would know
them . . . and they in turn would tell their children. Then they would put their trust in God
and would not forget his deeds but would keep
his commands.*   Psalm 78:4-7

God's plan for parents is that they set godly
standards and live them out before their children to ensure that their children follow the
ways of God. Today is a new day to begin being
all our family needs us to be.

> **Values are established early; our children depend on us.**

Train a child in the way he should go, and when he is old he will not turn from it. Proverbs 22:6

Many children grow up in godly homes and turn away from God. But the values they have been taught stay with them, and often in later life these values are the inducement that brings them back to God.

Correct discipline turns people
toward righteous living.

*Discipline your son, and he will give you peace;
he will bring delight to your soul.*   Proverbs 29:17

Discipline is more than spankings. It is the
application of standards and the meting out of
rewards as well as punishment. Our children
will be what we discipline them to be. God promises to help us today to discipline as he disciplines us—in love and wisdom.

Wise children are the product of
wise parents.

*My son, if your heart is wise, then my heart will
be glad; my inmost being will rejoice when your
lips speak what is right.*   Proverbs 23:15-16

Many times we are depressed to see reflected
in our children some of the mistakes we made
earlier in our life. God wants us today to begin
building strong family structures, which will be
a stabilizing effect not only in our life, but also
in theirs for generations to come.

God's promise to our children
will be fulfilled by the way
we live today.

All your sons will be taught by the Lord, and
great will be your children's peace.   Isaiah 54:13

To ensure the welfare of our children, we must
begin thinking about them now. During our
recovery, we tend to become self-centered, thinking of our own problems. We may not realize
how important our relationship to our children
is—to them and us. Accept God's promises to
help make today a new beginning of family building.

> **Good shown to others returns
> with blessing to us and
> praise to God.**

*For the Lord will be your confidence and will
keep your foot from being snared. Do not with-
hold good from those who deserve it, when it is
in your power to act.*   Proverbs 3:26-27

This command bears with it a promise from
God to bless us as we live honestly and generously with others. When we were struggling with
our past sins, we spent most of our time thinking
about ourselves and our own needs. A sign of
recovery is our being able and willing to begin
thinking of the welfare of others.

> **God blesses hard work—
> now and eternally.**

*Lazy hands make a man poor, but diligent hands
bring wealth. He who gathers crops in summer
is a wise son, but he who sleeps during harvest is
a disgraceful son.*   Proverbs 10:4-5

Sinful addictions launch us into a life-style
of procrastination "Tomorrow I'll do better".
Recovery puts us on the road to responsible
living. God blesses those who accept responsibility to be one who is consistently "giving" instead
of "taking" all the time.

> **Even when it hurts us to be
> honest, it is God's way of blessing.**

*The Lord abhors dishonest scales, but accurate
weights are his delight.*   Proverbs 11:1

When our life was out of control, we spent
much of our time thinking about our own
needs—and often very little time thinking
about how we were hurting others. A recovering
person assumes responsibility to be brutally
honest—with himself and with others. God's
promise for today is a day of blessing for a day
of honest living.

> God's best goes to the one
> who is satisfied with less of the
> world in order to have more
> of heaven's riches.

*Better a little with righteousness than much gain
with injustice.*   Proverbs 16:8

Once God begins to work in our life, as we
grow in our knowledge of him through prayer
and meditation on his Word, we gain better
perspective on what true wealth really is. Today
we must let God show us those things that have
eternal value.

When we leave our daily needs in
God's hands, he helps us to
escape the very temptations that
used to cause us to fall.

*He who walks righteously and speaks what is
right, who rejects gain from extortion and keeps
his hand from accepting bribes, who stops his
ears against plots of murder and shuts his eyes
against contemplating evil—this is the man who
will dwell on the heights, whose refuge will be
the mountain fortress. His bread will be supplied, and water will not fail him.*   Isaiah 33:15-16

Much of our past life of sin was spent taking
care of number one—ourselves. Now, today,
with God's blessing, we can confidently trust
him for everything we need and end the day with
a clear conscience.

> As we grow to be more
> Christlike, we look less and less
> like our old self.

*Do not lie to each other, since you have taken off
your old self with its practices and have put on
the new self, which is being renewed in knowledge in the image of its Creator.*   Colossians 3:9-10

Since we turned the control of our life over to
God, he has become our source of strength and
protection. We no longer need to lie and steal to
protect our own interests, since we now know
God can do a better job. Today, we must let God
work in us to make us more like him.

> **The call of God on our life is one
> of his greatest gifts.**

No one should wrong his brother or take advantage of him. The Lord will punish men for all such sins, as we have already told you and warned you. For God did not call us to be impure, but to live a holy life.   1 Thessalonians 4:6-7

Not only has God delivered us from a life of defeating and addicting sins; he has given us a purpose in life—to reflect his goodness to a world that needs the same freedom we have found. Today we must allow God to make us helpful—not harmful—to those around us.

Once we have received help, we
must become helpers.

*The wicked borrow and do not repay, but the
righteous give generously.*   Psalm 37:21

God calls it wicked for us to accept from
others without being willing to return the benefit
to the giver or to others. Once we have received
a degree of help in our recovery, we must act
responsibly toward others who need the kind of
help and encouragement we can give. God promises his blessing on us when we do.

> **Generosity is a sure sign of our understanding God's grace given to us.**

I was young and now I am old, yet I have never seen the righteous forsaken or their children begging bread. They are always generous and lend freely; their children will be blessed.

Psalm 37:25-26

Turning our life over to God and following his directions leads us into a path of blessing for ourselves, for our children, and for those around us. Grace given is grace to be shared. God's promise to us today is his blessing on us as we share his good gifts with others.

> **Obedience to God and concern
> for the welfare of others are
> closely linked.**

*Blessed is the man who fears the Lord, who finds
great delight in his commands. . . . Wealth and
riches are in his house, and his righteousness
endures forever. . . . He has scattered abroad
his gifts to the poor, his righteousness endures
forever; his horn will be lifted high in honor.*

Psalm 112:1, 3, 9

Today, we must trust God to make us as generous with others as he has been with us.

> We cannot outgive God—he
> always returns to us more than
> we can possibly give to others.

One man gives freely, yet gains even more;
another withholds unduly, but comes to poverty.
A generous man will prosper; he who refreshes
others will himself be refreshed.   Proverbs 11:24-25

God's benefits to us are not always measured
in dollars and cents. Yet, when we consider all
the ways God can add benefits to our life, we are
wise to allow him to show us today how much he
can bless us as we make the needs of others as
important as we consider our own to be.

> Everyone we meet today will see
> Jesus in us as we allow his life to
> be lived out in us.

He who is kind to the poor lends to the Lord,
and he will reward him for what he has done.

Proverbs 19:17

In a way we find hard to understand, the heart of God beats for all the needy people of the world. As we show kindness to them, God smiles, for that is what he would do if he dwelt in a flesh-and-blood body today. This wonderful promise is ours today: as we give to others, God will credit the benefit to our account, with interest!

Benefits given to us are benefits
to be shared.

*You will be made rich in every way so that you
can be generous on every occasion, and through
us your generosity will result in thanksgiving to
God.*   2 Corinthians 9:11

As God brings more light into our life, the
more we will realize how important to our recovery is the appreciation we show as we share with
others the Good News of a God who forgives and
restores broken lives.

❦

We are rich only if we acknowledge God as the giver of all good gifts.

Command those who are rich in this present world not to be arrogant nor to put their hope in wealth, which is so uncertain, but to put their hope in God, who richly provides us with everything for our enjoyment. Command them to do good, to be rich in good deeds, and to be generous and willing to share. 1 Timothy 6:17-18

This command bears the promise of God's blessing on those of us who realize God has given to us in order to enable us to share with others. We become truly rich not by getting, but by giving.

God, who interprets motives and
not amounts, knows the heart of
the generous giver.

*Each man should give what he has decided in his
heart to give, not reluctantly or under compul-
sion, for God loves a cheerful giver.*

2 Corinthians 9:7

We have struggled to become free from sins
that took much energy, and sometimes material
wealth, away from us. As God restores us to
sanity, he often restores us to usefulness. We
show how much we appreciate God's benefits
when we purpose in our heart to give. Generosity is measured not by how much we give, but by
the heart attitude with which the gift is given.